Praise for *Living Connected*

Afton Rorvik's heart beats in the rhythm of friendship. Her longing for deep connection has motivated her to help others struggling to find meaningful relationships. Her book *Living Connected* gives practical advice, insightful research, and biblical guidance all woven into her own honest stories. Women looking for help in cultivating friendship will find it here.

—**Sharla Fritz**, author of *Waiting: A Bible Study on Patience, Hope, and Trust*

At last—a field guide to friendship written by an especially keen observer of our human need for meaningful relationships! While tending and befriending others might come easily for the outgoing and gregarious among us, there are countless others whose empathy, loyalty, and generosity of spirit make them the kind of friends the rest of us long to have. Given their quiet, contemplative nature, how do those gifted with introversion establish mutually beneficial friendships in a world of noise and speed? Afton Rorvik has written a thoughtful, elegantly researched guide to friendship that will serve as a welcome companion to all those desiring to live in connection.

—**Maggie Wallem Rowe**, speaker and author of *This Life We Share*

Afton Rorvik *gets* me. If you're an introvert, she gets you too. She knows a bit about what it is to live in your skin. In *Living Connected*, Rorvik leads the reader down a path of discovery and self-understanding. I discovered grace to embrace how and who I am as well as fresh strategies to live well—and to live loved—as an introvert. No one who's an introvert should miss this book!

—**Margot Starbuck**, author of *The Grown Woman's Guide to Online Dating*

We all know we're called to love each other. But how? The truth is, we don't always know how to be a good friend—and who among us is brave enough to ask for help learning such a skill? In *Living Connected*, Afton Rorvik writes with honesty and clarity, drawing from her own wisdom to gently coach us on the journey to friendship. However skilled you may be at relationships, I'm confident you'll benefit from this heartfelt and practical guide.
—**Catherine McNiel**, author of *Fearing Bravely: Risking Love for Our Neighbors, Strangers, and Enemies*

You don't have to be an extrovert to have meaningful friendships! If you are an introvert, Afton Rorvik's *Living Connected* will help you make and grow authentic, healthy relational connections without becoming someone you're not.
—**David Horton**, former Editorial Director, Bethany House Publishers

In *Living Connected*, Afton Rorvik has created a guidebook out of the old adage "if you want to have a friend be a friend." This book takes some of the guesswork out of the complexity of friendship, particularly for introverts, like me, who might otherwise resort to just going it alone. And for extroverts, this book offers insight into the introvert mindset that might get in the way of meaningful friendship. In an age where loneliness has become epidemic, *Living Connected* is a must-read.
—**Charity Singleton Craig**, author of *The Art of the Essay*

You might not think an extrovert would enjoy a book about introverts and friendship, but then again, you might be wrong. I absolutely devoured Afton Rorvik's *Living Connected*. Not only did Rorvik remind me of the many important qualities in any good relationship—such as empathy, approachability, honesty, loyalty, humility, creativity, and generosity—but her words gave me greater understanding into people who are wired differently from me. I especially appreciated the practical application through journaling

prompts and sidebars. Let's face it, relationships and community are a priority for everyone today, so why not soak up wisdom from those who have learned the delicate dance of both coming together and time apart? If you're ready, *Living Connected* is a great place to start.
—**Lucinda Secrest McDowell**, award-winning author of *Soul Strong* and *Life-Giving Choices*

Living Connected is an engaging and practical guide to forming and maintaining emotionally healthy friendships. Afton specifically addresses introverts, but all personality types will benefit from both the writings and chapter journaling questions. An essential read!
—**Jennifer Stenzel**, MA, LCPC, Executive Director, Jennifer Stenzel Clinical Associates, Ltd.

As Afton Rorvik thoughtfully reminds us, "trust builds relationships." In a time when so many relationships are crumbling, how can we rebuild trust? With chapters on topics such as curiosity, confidentiality, and creativity, Living Connected provides useful scaffolding to help introverts (and extroverts too!) continue the crucial work of relational repair.
—**Melanie Weldon-Soiset**, poet, former pastor, and #ChurchToo spiritual abuse survivor

One strength of the book is how it is rooted in the thinking and reflection of others who have wrestled with friendship. Afton challenges and encourages her readers as she challenges and encourages herself. The book possesses a vulnerable tone, a hallmark of true friendship and evident in Afton's prose.
—**Dr. James H. Brownlee**, Associate Provost and Professor of English at Malone University

As a committed introvert, I love this book! Afton Rorvik names the challenges we face, validates our needs, and encourages us to bring our unique gifts to the world. If you're married to or friends with an introvert, *Living Connected* will help you to better understand how we tick. Anyone wanting to be a better friend will find encouragement and wisdom in this book.

—**Dorothy Littell Greco**, author of *Making Marriage Beautiful* and *Marriage in the Middle*

I have lived many of my eighty years without ever thinking about the challenge introverts face. In fact, when I did think or talk about introversion, it was usually with a negative slant—like this was a problem those introverts needed to solve! My good friend Afton Rorvik began to change that for me a few years ago, as she shared her life and writings with me. Now in this new book, she makes a powerful and persuasive case for the need and the resulting joy and strength that come from staying connected. Although she addresses it to introverts, It speaks to us outgoing extroverts just as much. In her wonderful storytelling style, she offers practical advice and suggestions on how to stay connected. Introvert or not—this is a book you need to read!

—**Mary Whelchel Lowman**, founder and speaker, The Christian Working Woman

Everyone should read this book! As a functional extrovert with an introvert's soul, I found *Living Connected* enlightening, entertaining, and immediately applicable. Extroverts will deepen their understanding of their more introverted friends. Introverts will learn the built-in strengths they can bring to every friendship and how to leverage these gifts to "live connected."

—**Stephen Maret**, PhD, Professor of Psychology, Nyack College

I loved the depth and breadth of Afton's exploration of friendship—and what gets in the way. Wise, transparent, funny, practical. I learned much, and so will you.

—**Elizabeth Cody Newenhuyse**, writer, speaker, semi-introvert

living connected

An Introvert's Guide to Friendship

afton rorvik

Imprint of Iron Stream Media

Birmingham, Alabama

Living Connected: An Introvert's Guide to Friendship

New Hope Publishers
100 Missionary Ridge
Birmingham, AL 35242
New Hope Publishers is an imprint of Iron Stream Media
NewHopePublishers.com
IronStreamMedia.com

© 2021 by Afton Rorvik

No part of this publication may be reproduced, stored in a retrieval system, or transmitted in any form or by any means—electronic, mechanical, photocopying, recording, or otherwise—without the prior written permission of the publisher.

Author is represented by the literary agency of Credo Communications, credocommunications.net.

While all the stories in this book are true, some of the details and names have been changed or deleted to protect the storyteller's identity. All stories are used by permission. Iron Stream Media serves its authors as they express their views, which may not express the views of the publisher.

Library of Congress Control Number: 2021940360

Unless otherwise indicated, all Scripture quotations are taken from the Holy Bible, New Living Translation, copyright © 1996, 2004, 2015 by Tyndale House Foundation. Used by permission of Tyndale House Publishers, Carol Stream, Illinois 60188. All rights reserved.

Scripture quotations marked MSG are taken from THE MESSAGE, copyright © 1993, 2002, 2018 by Eugene H. Peterson. Used by permission of NavPress, represented by Tyndale House Publishers. All rights reserved.

Scripture quotations marked (NIV) are taken from the Holy Bible, New International Version®, NIV®. Copyright © 1973, 1978, 1984, 2011 by Biblica, Inc.™ Used by permission of Zondervan. All rights reserved worldwide. www.zondervan.com The "NIV" and "New International Version" are trademarks registered in the United States Patent and Trademark Office by Biblica, Inc.™

Scripture quotations marked (TLB) are taken from The Living Bible copyright © 1971. Used by permission of Tyndale House Publishers, Carol Stream, Illinois 60188. All rights reserved.

ISBN: 978-1-56309-536-8 (paperback)

ISBN: 978-1-56309-537-5 (ebook)

1 2 3 4 5—25 24 23 22 21

Printed in the United States of America

DEDICATION

To Mudder
Your gift of approaching people inspires me.
Your deep faith in God and your determination
to practice gratitude do too.

To Mom
You claimed the title of "introvert" but still
managed to have "700 friends."
I watched and learned and marveled. Grateful!

Contents

Acknowledgments 11
Preface 15
Introduction 17
1. Honesty 23
2. Generosity 41
3. Approachability 59
4. Curiosity 77
5. Empathy 95
6. Loyalty 113
7. Confidentiality 133
8. Consistency 153
9. Flexibility 171
10. Creativity 189
11. Hospitality 207
12. Humility 225
Notes 239
Resources 251

Acknowledgments

This book contains so many stories of people I hold dear. How I love sharing these stories and these people with you.

Thank you, Roberta Choma, for reaching out to me in junior high and hanging on to me even now. How I admire your gift of loyalty.

And thank you to my BCM friends from college—Linda Baker, Jacqui Harmeling, Jody Lubenec, and honorary member Karen Riley—your friendship and your faith inspired me then and still inspire me now. I practice hospitality because of you. Thank you for letting me share you and your inspiring stories here.

Thank you to my brothers for cheering me on in this writing life.

Thank you, extended family, sisters- and brothers-in-law, nephews, and nieces, for discovering with me the joy of growing together. A special thank you to Mudder, Tom, Ellen, Marianne, and Sarah for sharing your stories within this book.

Thank you, Bev Fishleigh, for the gift of friendship just outside my door.

Thank you, neighbors, for making ours a connected neighborhood. You have taught me so much.

Thank you, Sharla Fritz, for reading every word of this book and offering wise suggestions and thoughtful stories. How I treasure our connection through words.

Thank you, women of the Redbud Writers Guild, for sharing this writing journey of faith with me. Your wisdom, prayers, encouragement, and challenge have meant so much to me. Sharla Fritz, Lara Krupicka, Dorothy Littell Greco, Nilwona Nowlin, Melody Latrice Copenny, Jenny McGill, Carlene Hill Byron, Catherine McNiel, Aubrey Sampson, Mary Anderson, April Yamasaki, JoHannah Reardon, Belinda Bauman, Marlena Graves, and Leslie Verner, thank you especially for helping shape this book with your wisdom and stories.

Thank you to "Saki's" family for letting Roberta and me remember her through story.

Thank you to all not mentioned above who gifted me with your stories, including Suzanne Alexander, Anna, Jayne Wilson Bowman, Amy House Flood, Peggy Ingram, Chris Mazzerella, Michelle, Falecia Sanchez, Patty Spence, Jennifer Stenzel, and countless others who chose to remain unnamed. You all inspire and challenge me.

Thank you, early readers, for reading these chapters as I wrote them and offering comments and some of your own thoughtful stories: Linda Baker, Melody Bodger, Roberta Choma, John Choma, Ruth Dykstra, and Lara Krupicka. You have made this book so much stronger. How I appreciate the gifts of your time and honesty!

Thank you to my agent Karen Neumair for believing in this idea and helping me shape it. I so appreciate your vision and challenge. Thank you, Ramona Richards and Susan Cornell, for your wise and careful editing all while preserving my voice. And thank you to Kim McCulla and the many other people behind the scenes at Iron Stream Media.

Thank you to my endorsers for helping me send this book out into the world.

Thank you, Karen Allen and Peg Knight, for understanding my need for time and space to write and

Acknowledgments

think. And thank you, Christine Hart, Imani Todd, Jean Uzumecki, and others who took shifts for me.

Thank you to my children, Karl and Annalisa, for learning with me about living connected. I celebrate the remarkable people you are and love you more than words could ever say. And Karolina, I'm thankful for you every day.

Thank you especially to John, my extroverted husband, who has helped me see and own my quiet voice, helped me find the courage to pursue writing this book, and liberally gifted me with his humor and stories along the way. I love you deeply and love this connected life we have built together!

Thank you, God, for wiring me as an introvert. I cherish this gift.

Preface

How do we make and keep friends? And how do we who call ourselves introverts step outside our quiet worlds and reach for others?

I have wrestled with these questions for decades and read everything I could find about friendship (that is what we introverts do). I have also promised myself that I will work on friendships. They breathe life and color into my life. My friends provide balance and perspective. They keep me honest. They help me fight depression.

Some of you might come from families where relationships inside and outside the family just seemed to add layer upon layer of stress. You may have concluded that relationships of any type just don't seem worth the effort. You haven't seen any that give you hope.

Or maybe you find yourself in the thick of busy years with a career and/or family. You scarcely have time to sleep. And yet you long for some time to spend with a friend. You vaguely remember that you used to enjoy that.

Perhaps you, like me, have an empty nest and suddenly have more time for yourself and for friendships.

Wherever you find yourself on the road to building friendships, you will find encouragement and practical thinking here. And maybe even a few laughs.

After the publication of my first book, *Storm Sisters*, in 2014, I received emails and comments on social media from many readers who said something that surprised me: "I like the idea of a Storm Sister, a friend who sticks around when life gets hard, but before I find that Storm Sister, I need to have a sister, a friend. How do I do that? How do I find friends?"

Headlines in our news about the raging epidemic of loneliness throughout our world echo these comments from my readers. And the COVID-19 pandemic certainly added an additional layer to that epidemic of loneliness.

The day I signed the contract for this book in March 2020, our state government issued a stay-at-home proclamation because of the COVID-19 virus. What irony to write about friendship in a climate of isolation and social distancing!

As I wrote these chapters, I wondered how this pandemic period of social isolation would affect our lonely world. Would we simply adjust and adapt to living socially distant? Or would we realize at the core of our beings what a gift we have in real-life connection and become even more committed than ever to pursuing relationships? Only time will tell.

Oh, how I hope we will become people who hunger for and pursue real-life connection. Even we introverts!

I have come to believe in friendship as one of God's greatest gifts. And so, I wrote this book to peel off some of the wrapping paper on God's good gift of friendship and help you start enjoying it as I have.

Thanks for joining me on this pursuit to live connected. Cheering you on!

Introduction

For most of my life, I have viewed my "quiet soul" as a liability.

When I discovered Susan Cain's profoundly thoughtful book *Quiet*, I began to think differently about my introversion. In fact, I began to see my introversion as a gift, particularly in the area of building friendships. What a surprise!

And then I went on to read Adam McHugh's book, *Introverts in the Church: Finding Our Place in an Extroverted Culture*. I underlined liberally and nodded my head often. I particularly like his definition of introverts: "If your preference is toward your inner world, and even when you are out socializing you are thinking of a quiet place, you win the label 'introvert.'"[1]

For too long I shoved aside my natural, introverted ways and tried to imitate my extroverted friends. Now, rather than trying to ignore my introversion, I recognize it, embrace it, and make changes in my life that accommodate and even enrich it. I feel better!

I don't write this book as an expert with all the answers; rather, I write this book as a fellow traveler, learning as I go about living connected as an introvert.

When I type the word *introvert* into a search engine on my computer, I see funny cartoons about people having a wonderful night in or people having a strong aversion to talking on the phone. I laugh and nod my head. But then I also see T-shirts and Pinterest quotations that display some version of "I'm an introvert. Go away!" Those images make me wince. On one hand, I agree. Living next to people presents challenges and inevitable conflicts. On the other hand, I believe my faith in God calls me to live connected.

I see the power of connection in the Book of Nehemiah as the people of Jerusalem worked *together* to restore their city. I see it in the story of the paralyzed man whose friends brought him to the feet of Jesus for healing as recorded in Mark 2. I see it in 1 Corinthians 12 as Paul described the many parts of the human body to illustrate the connectedness of believers in God.

I can't ignore God's powerful call to living connected. I also can't ignore my internal wiring as an introvert.

So how do I live connected while also living well as an introvert?

I wrestle with this question. Daily.

Of course, I set out to answer this question introvert-style, which included reading a lot of books. I returned to one of the first books I read on friendship: *The Friendship Factor* by Alan Loy McGinnis, published in 1979 and still in print today. I also read books and blogs by current writers.

And I had a lot of one-on-one conversations with people, including my husband and favorite extrovert. He knows that quiet fuels me. I know that people-activity fuels him. We give each other space, time, and respect to grow and live. And we've worked to find common ground. (And yes, we had some adjusting to do when his job moved home during our shelter-in-place order. But that's another story.) We both greatly value our friendship with each other and our friendships with others. We speak often of friendships and how to nurture them. Much of what appears in this book first began as a discussion with John.

Introduction

As a result of those discussions in combination with reading, thinking, and praying about my own quiet soul, I've landed on some words that I want to incorporate into my own friendships, words that help me follow God's call to connect: honesty, generosity, approachability, curiosity, empathy, loyalty, confidentiality, consistency, flexibility, creativity, hospitality, and humility.

Some of these words represent great challenge for me. And I bungle friendship all the time. (Just ask my friends!) But I do hold these words in my head and heart and want them to shape the way I connect, even as an introvert.

- **Honesty**—Francesca Batestelli sings a song titled "If We're Honest" in which she repeats a line: "I'm a mess and so are you." What would our friendships look like if we adopted this way of thinking?
- **Generosity**—We introverts can easily get sucked into toxic friendships where we listen most and give most. How would our friendships change and thrive with a mutual mix of openhandedness and openheartedness?
- **Approachability**—My mother-in-law can (and does) talk to anyone. I admire her for it! Walking into a room full of strangers can make me want to run and hide under a blanket. And yet, I have to do this for work and for the sake of those I love who host parties and other events. How can we introverts learn to initiate connections in a quiet, thoughtful sort of way?
- **Curiosity**—Often introverts excel at curiosity. In fact, many of us long for an off switch for our brains that constantly observe and process.

How can we tap into our natural abilities and build connections through asking thoughtful questions?

- **Empathy**—Because we introverts tend to listen well and think deeply, empathy often comes naturally for us. How can we hone this ability and use it to breathe life into relationships in this age of "me-first"?
- **Loyalty**—These days we mostly use the word *loyalty* to talk about a brand not a friendship. How can we wisely learn to exercise loyalty, but not loyalty at any cost, in relationships?
- **Confidentiality**—Because we introverts tend to spend so much time thinking and processing information before we actually speak, we hold a distinct advantage in the confidentiality department. How and when should we exercise confidentiality as a friendship-building tool?
- **Consistency**—Who of us would not want a friend who says, "When I tell you I will do something with/for you, I will definitely do it. You can count on me"? Introverts often thrive with schedules and routines and can learn quickly the value of acting with predictability in a friendship.
- **Flexibility**—We introverts, who don't tend to think well on our feet, may struggle greatly with practicing flexibility. I do. How might our friendships grow if we decided to make practicing flexibility a lifetime pursuit?
- **Creativity**—God has drenched our world with color and creativity, something introverts tend to value deeply. How might our love of creativity spill over into relationships and revive or jump-start them?
- **Hospitality**—Introverts often feel on the fringe,

Introduction

especially in a room full of people. What might happen if we tapped into our natural empathy and let it propel us toward others who feel the same way?

- **Humility**—We introverts can so easily feel less-than, especially in social situations. But what if we truly understood and accepted how God wired us and loved us? How then could we reach out and connect with others?

As my college English professor used to say, "Come with me on this journey!"

Chapter 1

Honesty

I'm a mess and so are you.
—Francesca Battistelli

I didn't mean to say anything; it just popped out of my mouth.

John and I had agreed to meet some friends for lunch, and we had covered the usual topics of jobs and family and vacations. And then, in the middle of dessert, my pain related to a family member's choices spilled out of my mouth.

Splat! Right in the middle of the table and right in the middle of our friendship with this couple.

I wanted to push rewind. I wanted to run out of the restaurant. I wanted to rush on to another topic. But I also felt so weary of pretending everything was "fine." I just couldn't do it anymore.

John gulped, and we exchanged nervous glances. How would our friends react? Would they find polite ways to back out of future invitations to dinner? Would they feel overwhelmed?

Confront This Age of Image Management

Why do we worry so much about how others perceive us?

Maybe we want people to think well of us. Maybe we do not want to "burden" anyone.

Living Connected

Maybe we have absorbed the social-media vibe of portraying ourselves in the best possible light at all times.

Image management. We want people to see our best selves.

But how can we develop deep, life-giving friendship if we never get below the surface conversations about work and weather and vacations? If we never reveal our imperfect, not-so-social-media-worthy selves?

A friend shared with me her journey of learning to let go of her need to appear fine. It all started with a self-revelatory conversation she had with a friend.

> My friend has been through the journey of grief, of loved ones taken too soon. Her family has been deeply impacted by addiction. She has also experienced the chaos of finances turning her world upside-down and the emotional impact on her heart and on the hearts of those she loves.
>
> As a result, a flame is ignited in the heart of my friend and her husband, as they lead a faith-based recovery group—a small band of those willing to honestly exchange their heartache for healing.
>
> The flame grows as it is passed to others.
>
> One morning, over breakfast, I received the torch. She handed it off after I finally unlocked the secret I had carefully hidden for years: a challenging marriage that I was totally unprepared to handle. All I knew was to hide it, to cover it up with appearances, and to sacrifice my sanity and my soul in the process. While trying to hold everything together—my marriage, my family, my faith—the secret tore me apart. The paste of appearance is unreliable, ineffective, and ultimately, corrosive.
>
> My friend's words, "You are codependent," and her direct advice to join a recovery group launched me on a path toward healing friendships and personal integrity.
>
> I am forever grateful that she honestly shared her story with me. She then became a safe harbor for me to finally forsake the bondage of my secret.

Since that time, I have been learning to pass the torch of honesty myself. As a member of a support group, I've made the choice to be vulnerable to others by sharing my story. I've noticed that after I open up, it encourages another person to take the risk of authenticity.

The flame is strengthened and fueled. Ready to pass . . . again.[1]

Honesty, self-revelation, however you choose to describe it, these words represent a more than slightly terrifying concept. And yet living out this concept changes lives. Again and again.

Fight the Urge to Overshare

Before we look closely at ways to let down our guard and use self-revelatory words to build friendships, let's pause and consider what happens when someone overshares personal information.

If I filled up a large pitcher with water and then emptied it on a tiny basil plant sitting on my kitchen windowsill, my plant would complain by developing yellow leaves. Too much water!

Sometimes in friendships we can overwater, can't we? We pour out the details of our lives in a great rush when we sense we have a listening ear.

Confession here: I have overwatered both plants and friendships.

When my freshman-year roommate and I sat down to talk through the list of get-to-know-you questions, I spilled my soul and talked about my pain at length. She listened well. Sadly, I can't tell you what she said that afternoon.

In that moment I longed for a friend. Far from home and thrust onto a college campus with people I didn't know, my introverted self felt desperate for a connection, just one friend. What better way to connect than to share my soul? All of it. All at once.

I have learned by doing and failing and doing again over many years that friendships thrive best with bits of water (many times of connection) over the long haul. Self-revelation, yes, but in doses. And in approximately equal measures from both friends.

Dr. John Townsend says it well in his book *How to Be a Best Friend Forever*: "Attachment among best friends works best when both people are vulnerable and open, and make that vulnerability a normal part of the friendship. This is important because without mutual vulnerability, one person becomes the counselor and the other the counselee, which is not the true nature of friendship. Friendship is always a two-way street."[2]

When I unloaded on my unsuspecting college roommate, I talked to her as I would a counselor—all about me. But she had not signed up to serve as my personal counselor; she had simply signed up to live with me as a friend.

How often, I wonder, do we approach friendship with the hope that we will find a personal counselor?

Finding that sweet spot of not too much but just enough self-revelation in a friendship can feel like a dance. Sometimes we need to throttle ourselves; sometimes we need to take a deep breath and speak an honest sentence about a current struggle.

How can we know when to say what? And why bother? Why not just take a nap?

Introverts have a distinct advantage in the self-revelatory friendship dance. We can't help analyzing situations and people; it just comes with the territory of an always-active mind. When we listen to our brains and combine our knowledge with our intuition, we find courage to take a step toward friendship.

Honesty

Ask Yourself Some Honest Questions

As we learn the dance of friendship and seek to present our true selves to others, the more we know about ourselves the better we will become at sharing bits of our true selves with others. And the more we know and understand ourselves, the better chance we have of developing healthy relationships.

So who are you? In real life, not just on social media. Let's take a look at some key questions.

What energizes you?

Many employers ask potential prospects to take personality tests, aimed at helping companies determine if this person would fit well in a specific role. Obviously, no test, no category, can completely define a person, but they can open our eyes.

Susan Cain does a marvelous job of explaining the nuances of two types of people—introverts and extroverts—in her book *Quiet*: "Introverts feel 'just right' with less stimulation, as when they sip wine with a close friend, solve a crossword puzzle, or read a book. Extroverts enjoy the extra bang that comes from activities like meeting new people, skiing slippery slopes, and cranking up the stereo."[3]

As an introverted lawyer herself, she found that she could feel intimidated and "not enough" when surrounded by a room full of extroverts. She talks honestly of her journey to own her personality and see it as a positive.

Over tea recently, a perceptive friend pointed out to me that I had dodged her question by asking her a question and then settling in for a good listen: "You're doing that introvert thing where you ask questions and listen."

Busted! Conversation takes effort for me—more than it does for my extroverted friends who bubble over with enthusiasm and insights. So, to keep my friendships from becoming counseling sessions, I need to listen *less* sometimes and force myself to talk *more*.

Do you know where you fall on the introvert/extrovert spectrum? And in friendships do you need to push yourself to talk more or talk less? What else have you learned about your personality from tests such as the Myers Briggs Type Indicator or the Enneagram Test?

> **Introvert Inclinations**
> Draw energy from quiet and alone time.
> Often have an active mind.
>   ("I've been thinking . . .")
> Prefer "going deep" to small talk.

How do you communicate best?

I have an awkward relationship with phones.

I really don't know how it started. Maybe the party line we had in my growing-up years? Maybe my introverted self really needs body language to find courage to talk. And I always wonder if my phone call will interrupt someone in the middle of an important meeting at work or in an intense family discussion.

Several years ago, I set my ring tone to quack like a duck because otherwise, out in public, I just ignored the normal, factory-preset ringtone, assuming it rang for someone else. Truthfully, the harsh quack of my phone mirrors how I feel about it. Every time it rings—"quack, quack, quack"—I jump. The harsh sound scares me, but I also worry, truly, about what I will hear when I answer the phone.

How ridiculous!

Honesty

And yet I must honestly admit to myself that I just don't like talking on the phone. I would so much rather text or email. When I communicate through a text or email, I have time to craft my words carefully and say precisely what I need to say without stumbling and saying something stupid.

But I have several friends who love to talk on the phone. They graciously call me periodically, knowing that I probably will not call them but will send an email or text.

As I write this, a new year has begun, and I hear a lot about New Year's resolutions. Some choose a word they want to define their year. Some want to get healthy. Some want to read the Bible in a year. My goal? I want to work on calling my "I-love-talking-on-the-phone" friends more, not forcing them to make all the effort to stay in touch.

Sigh. This feels embarrassing. This feels hard.

It also feels right. These people matter to me. I want to connect with them. I want to know their stories. I cannot expect that they will always communicate with me the way I feel most comfortable. I have to work at this.

Communication matters so much in building friendships, doesn't it? What is your go-to communication method? And do you know your friends' go-to communication methods? Can you adapt as needed sometimes? And can you have an honest conversation with friends about how you communicate best?

What do you love?

After my mom died and I returned home to my family and friends, I couldn't remember what I had loved doing. So much of my time and effort had gone into days and months of thinking about my mom and what she needed that I had lost myself. A wise counselor encouraged me to make a list of things I loved and do one thing on that list every day.

Seems egocentric to think about what I love to do, but if I don't think about it, then I simply get swept up into other people's preferences and become the person they need. That, again, feels more like the counselor/counselee relationship.

Any relationship involves two people—two voices. Both voices matter. If you have the quieter voice, you may feel kind and loving in letting your voice take second place. But, in truth, by concealing or burying your voice, you foster dishonesty in your relationship. Your friend will struggle to know the real you.

I married a man with strong opinions about all sorts of things. Just last night he said, "How could anyone not like chocolate pudding? Isn't this your favorite dessert?"

Truthfully, no. In fact, I would rather have a large plate of green beans.

Owning what I love and speaking it aloud has taken effort for me. Not so much for John. He has graciously learned to ask me frequently, "What do you love?"

Dr. Gary Chapman wrote a fabulous, best-selling book all about that question and how it impacts relationships.[4] Knowing what you love matters as does using your words to state what you love in the context of a friendship (and in a marriage). And, of course, listening to what your friend loves matters too.

What family-of-origin pain do you carry with you?

We all grew up in imperfect families and learned imperfect habits. I grew up in a home where fear and anger ruled. Whether we want to admit it or not, our families of origin shape the current version of ourselves

Honesty

and our relationships. The more we understand and acknowledge our family-of-origin pain, the better we can forge strong, authentic friendships.

In her thoughtful book *Making Marriage Beautiful*, author Dorothy Greco explains: "Not long after we were married, Christopher and I started having conflicts about what it meant to be home in time for dinner." They did the dance of anger and apology but kept returning to the subject until Dorothy took an honest look at her past.

> During my middle and high school years, dinner could be a tense affair. *Would Dad be on time? Would he be sober? If he wasn't, how would Mom respond?* There was an obvious connection between my childhood wounds and our marital strife. Christopher's struggle with time management uncovered my unresolved pain and amplified my unprocessed anger. My response replicated my family of origin's patterns and certainly did not help Christopher feel loved or grow in his time management skills.[5]

If you have never taken a long, honest look at your growing-up years, please do. Otherwise, you will carry that pain and frustration into current relationships, repeating unhealthy patterns.

What challenges you?

For most of my life I have shamed myself about facing challenging social situations. I have muttered to myself some version of, "Oh, come on! Don't let fear win. Just do this. You have to. Other people do it!"

As an introvert, I thrive in quiet. Spending time at home alone suits me just fine. In fact, it makes my heart sing. Attending a neighborhood block party, a family reunion, a dinner party with people I don't know well, or job training in another facility where I don't normally work all make my heart pound. Truly.

We introverts have so much going on in our brains that we can struggle to corral and organize those thoughts into a coherent sentence, especially in a loud, unfamiliar environment. The whole process can make us feel utterly exhausted and in great need of a long nap.

In a delightful episode of the *New York Times* podcast *The Daily*, "A Special Episode for Kids: The Fear Facer", nine-year-old Ella Maners talks candidly about her own particular, paralyzing fears of throwing up and tornadoes and her Obsessive Compulsive Disorder (OCD). She also describes a Fear Facers summer camp where she learned to face (and talk to) her fears.

Ella named her OCD "Ocie" and says she imagines him or her as a blue bubble inside her brain—a sneaky blue bubble because she doesn't know what he or she will do.[6]

Ella seems to have discovered that speaking the truth about how she feels deflates rather than inflates the fear; in fact, it pops the blue bubble of fear.

I have discovered the same thing. Telling myself, *Just suck it up, get over yourself, and do what an extrovert would do*, doesn't work. But telling myself the truth about how I feel in a situation (or about an upcoming situation), based on my introverted personality, does work.

My friend Sharla recently had a significant birthday. Her sister noticed from Facebook that I knew Sharla, so she messaged me and invited me to a surprise birthday party at a local restaurant. I knew that I would know no one except my friend and her husband. For several days I formulated excuses: busy time of year, big writing project, not feeling great . . . And then I had a serious talk with myself: *Sharla is your friend. You want to cele-*

Honesty

brate her. And meet her people and learn more about her. This matters. You need to show up. And so I RSVP'd YES.

I also let myself say aloud, "This will be hard! I will feel uncomfortable."

And I formulated a plan, complete with some questions to ask other guests. Additionally, I gave myself permission to leave early. And I gave myself permission to take multiple long bathroom breaks to recalibrate in silence.

I enjoyed the event! Speaking honest words to myself about the social challenge I faced made all the difference.

So, what challenges you?

> **Introvert Impediments**
> Struggle to find the right word at the right time to express complicated, inner thoughts.
> Settle in to listen and forget to work at talking.
> Often find the phone a challenging way to communicate.

Use Self-Knowledge as Fuel for Friendships

Understanding ourselves can lay the foundation for self-revelation, a powerful friendship-building tool. Sadly, however, we often use our personality quirks as an excuse not to make the effort of reaching out to people. Consider these scenarios.

> I'm an introvert. I'm just not really good at social events. I think I'll just stay home.
> *versus*
> I'm an introvert. Social events challenge me, but I need to meet new people so I will come up with

a strategy (connect with one person, go with a friend, attend for just an hour) that works for me.

My new acquaintance loves to go to loud, expensive restaurants, but the whole experience wears me out. I guess we are just not meant to be friends.
versus
I'm grateful that this person wants to spend time with me. I will suggest that we order something from a restaurant and then bring the food to my (quiet) house to eat.

I just keep ignoring this person who calls on the phone. He calls at the worst times. And I'm afraid I'll say something stupid if I answer his phone call.
versus
I know this person wants to reach me but talking on the phone is hard for me. I'll text him and set up a specific time to talk on the phone, and I will have a list of talking points in front of me.

My friend just won't listen to me the way I want her to. She seems more focused on getting stuff done. Guess I'll just give up on this relationship. Not worth the continued disappointment.
versus
This friend reminds me a lot of my mom, who was always so busy with her job that I just couldn't get her to listen to me. I need to realize that my friend is not my mother. And I need to find a way to tell my friend about some of my pain related to my mom.

On business trips I have to go to networking events. I don't like the crowded, loud atmosphere, but I just have to suck it up if I want to keep my job.
versus

> I don't really like networking events—all the noise and small talk with people I don't know well. I will consider asking to meet one or two colleagues for dinner instead or attending the event for a short amount of time or telling colleagues I just need some downtime now, but I could meet for breakfast.

Learning to practice honesty with ourselves should help us enter more confidently into challenging situations. Self-awareness helps us say, *I can do this in my own unique, introverted way,* rather than saying, *This just feels too hard. Why bother?*

Practice Self-Revelation with Someone Who Loves You as You Are

Even those of us who happily spend hours alone with our minds and our books need friends. The days of stay-at-home during COVID-19 showed me that so vividly. When I don't connect with other people on a regular basis, I sink into myself and depression lurks. The scary world looks ominous. My little piece of the story looms large.

But when I connect with other people and hear their stories, I realize that I don't navigate this scary moment alone. People see and care.

Most of us would so love to have a friend (or a spouse) who could practically read our mind and know just how to encourage and comfort and challenge. A 24/7 friend.

But no person, no matter how thoughtful, can ever provide all that we need all the time. Only God can and does do that.

Living Connected

We cause ourselves a lot of pain because we often expect from a friend what only God can give.

As a teenager I discovered the Book of Psalms in the Bible:

> Lord, have mercy on me; all day long the enemy troops press in. So many are proud to fight against me; how they long to conquer me.
>
> But when I am afraid, I will put my confidence in you. Yes, I will trust the promises of God. And since I am trusting him, what can mere man do to me? They are always twisting what I say. All their thoughts are how to harm me. They meet together to perfect their plans; they hide beside the trail, listening for my steps, waiting to kill me. They expect to get away with it. Don't let them, Lord. In anger cast them to the ground.
>
> You have seen me tossing and turning through the night. You have collected all my tears and preserved them in your bottle! You have recorded every one in your book. (Psalm 56:1–8 TLB)

These words surprised me in their utter honesty. Nothing "fine" here. Lots of raw emotion. Lots of fear. And apparently the author could talk to God this way and not get struck by divine lightning.

I decided to read more of the Psalms. And the more I read, the more honesty and self-revelation I saw. And then I learned that one of the authors behind these honest bits of writing had committed adultery and murder.

The more I read the Psalms, the more I began to borrow these words to express the ache of my own heart. I realized that God could handle my rough, raw emotions and help me through them. And I realized that God loved me. Rough, raw, introverted me. Remarkable!

And now, many decades later, I make it a point to sit in my comfortable chair almost every morning and connect with God through listening to worship music, prayer, and reading the Bible. I open my heart to Him and confess my worries, failures, self-doubt, and fears, and I ask Him to open my eyes to see both my own heart and the hearts of others.

This time with God has become the fuel that starts my day. When I spend my morning time with God, I enter into the day feeling loved and heard. God has filled my tank with His love. I then have energy to reach out to other people. If I don't fuel my soul with God-time, however, I inevitably seek other loves to fuel my soul, including friends.

Go First

When I opened my mouth and spilled a bit of my pain to our friends at lunch many years ago, I knew that moment of self-revelation would define the direction of our friendship. It could serve as a roadblock: *We just can't go "there."* It could serve as an irritation, either lasting or temporary: *Really? We were having so much fun talking about vacations. Let's get back to talking about fun things.* Or it could function as a life-altering detour: *Tell us more. We will go "there" with you.*

After what seemed like a very long silence that particular afternoon, one of our friends said softly, "We are going through something similar."

I had no idea. I thought everything in their lives was fine. They seemed so together. And they smiled a lot.

That awkward, honest, in-the-middle-of-dessert moment led to a friendship that has grown steadily over the years. Our friends "went there" with us. We have now come to know each other well enough that we can say to each other, "If you need us to come at two in the morning, we will come."

What about you? Do you feel willing and able to mention one or two self-revelatory, honest bits to an acquaintance and lay the foundation for a potential friendship?

> **Challenge Your Introverted Self**
> Think of someone you know a bit but would like to know on a deeper level. Consider a neighbor, a coworker, the parent of one of your child's friends, a sister-in-law, brother-in-law, a cousin. Given your unique personality, how can you add one bit of self-revelation to this relationship?

Perhaps you have made gestures of connection in the past with someone and watched as that person erected a roadblock or grimaced and changed the subject or gossiped about your struggle behind your back to someone else.

Not everyone has the courage and stamina to learn the dance of friendship. Keep looking for those people who do, those people who can say truthfully, "I'm a mess and so are you." Don't give up on friendship because of some painful misfires. Instead, commit yourself to learning this rigorous dance with such rich rewards.

And read on to discover how generosity, living open-handed and openhearted can nurture friendships.

Journaling Questions

Before you read the next chapter on generosity, take some time to think about the role of honesty and self-revelation in your life and friendships.

Honesty

1. How do you react to that word *honesty* in connection with friendships?
2. Do you tend to "overwater" friendships with too much self-revelation? Describe a situation.
3. Or do you "underwater" friendships by keeping most of your thoughts and feelings to yourself? Describe a situation.
4. How have you worked at knowing yourself? What more can you do?
5. Who in your life has taken honest, self-revelatory steps toward you? How did you react? What did you learn from this experience?
6. Do you have an honest, self-revelatory relationship with God? If not, how might you begin to cultivate this? If so, how does this relationship provide you fuel for building other relationships?

Chapter 2

Generosity

If Nature has made you for a giver, your hands are born open, and so is your heart; and though there may be times when your hands are empty, your heart is always full, and you can give things out of that—warm things, kind things, sweet things—help and comfort and laughter.

—Frances Hodgson Burnett

By December 2005 I knew Mom didn't have long in this world. Her Creutzfeldt-Jakob disease, diagnosed only a month earlier, had started chewing up her brain with a vengeance. I tried to spend as much time in Colorado with her as I could but also tried to care for my own family. I felt so stretched.

On one of my pop-ins home, a friend called and said, "I have tickets for the opera. Would you and your daughter like to go?"

Yes! Oh, yes!

And so my daughter and I went with this friend and her daughter to a fabulous performance of *The Magic Flute* at Lyric Opera. I lost myself in the thrill of the higher-than-I-could-ever-sing aria of the Queen of the Night. I laughed out loud at Papageno's happy flute ditty and silly aria. I forgot for a moment my impending loss of my mother and remembered instead the woman who had often turned on the Saturday noon radio broadcast of the New York Metropolitan Opera.

The next day after the performance I went to a store and bought two CDs of the opera—one for me and one for my generous friend. And then I headed back to the airport and back to my opera-loving mother.

As she declined, I gasped for breath. I wanted to be with her and yet I had never done anything so hard. I reached for something that she loved—opera. Every morning as I left her house, driving her stick-shift Honda, I popped in my *Magic Flute* CD and cranked the volume.

I don't remember saying much to my friend about my mom that night at the opera. I do remember the price on the bottom of my ticket.

Ten years after that night at the opera with my friend, I saw a local college production of *The Magic Flute*. Once again, I lost myself in the magnificent and silly arias and much to my surprise I had to wipe tears from my eyes as I remembered the generous gift of opera years earlier.

I know that my friend did not sit down and say to herself, *Afton told me once her mother loved opera, so I think taking her to one would be really helpful right now as her mother is dying.* I don't even remember if I had told her my mom was deathly sick. And if she had asked me, *How can I help you as you grieve the impending death of your mom?* I would not have said, *Take me to an opera.* The idea would never have even popped into my head.

My friend simply opened her hand and her heart (and her wallet) to me and offered to share something she loved with me.

How it spoke to my aching heart.

Practice Generosity of Heart and Hand

Way back in the days of knights in shining armor the word *generosity* described someone of noble birth, an elite member of society.[1] Obviously, we don't still use the word that way, and we don't have knights dashing around. These days we use *generosity* mostly to describe someone's kind action, like treating a friend to the opera, or in my husband's case, a baseball game.

But generosity doesn't merely describe an action, does it? The word also describes an attitude. Frances Hodgson Burnett described it this way in *A Little Princess*: "If Nature has made you for a giver, your hands are born open, and so is your heart."[2]

We define *generosity* today with some of these synonyms: *bigheartedness, largesse, munificence, openhandedness, openheartedness,* and *unselfishness*.[3]

I particularly like the word *openhandedness*. If I have an open hand, I can't hold things well. I also can't keep secret things hidden in my hand. And if I let go of things or secrets, I usually do it because my heart leads the way. *Openhandedness* and *openheartedness* act like newborn twins, who thrive when connected.

We can easily focus on the hand part of generosity and neglect the heart part. After all, God told us, "Do to others what you would have them do to you" (Matthew 7:12 NIV). DO, DO, DO. And we can measure how much we do. We can see it: *I sent a card and a donation for funeral expenses; I mowed my elderly neighbor's lawn.*

When I speak about the idea of living as Storm Sisters, people seem to gravitate toward discussing the practical things we can do for a grieving friend. I have heard some wonderfully creative ideas. And I have met some very kind, busy, thoughtful people. They often also seem exhausted. I fear that they think they have to do it all for a sick friend. I see it in them because I also see it in myself.

So as we learn together about practicing generosity, let us remember that true generosity requires equal measures of heart and hand. And when practiced with balance, generosity helps build a foundation for strong, healthy, life-giving friendship.

Avoid the Tendency to Overgive

I often joke that I have never met a potato chip I didn't like. I could probably say the same about a cup of flavored coffee. But I have come to realize that if I eat half of a family-size bag of chips, I will get a severe stomachache. And if I guzzle a pot of caffeinated, flavored coffee after noon, I will find myself staring at my bedroom ceiling at 3 a.m. Too much of a good thing!

So what happens in a relationship, a potential friendship, when generosity becomes too much?

Let's face it, we like to rescue. We like to fix. We like to take on the role of hero. But if we step in and mount a rescue with our generosity, we just might deprive a friend of the satisfaction of succeeding on his or her own. Great growth and strength come from struggle.

And, honestly, sometimes we think we can buy friendship. *If I do enough or give enough to this person, certainly then she will feel as if she should pay attention to me.*

Clearly, generosity gone overboard does NOT build healthy relationships, so before we embark on understanding and implementing generosity in our friendships, let's make sure we know the difference between true generosity and overgiving.

Generosity

Writer and social worker Karen Kleiman offers some statements that identify overgiving tendencies. Maybe you see yourself in these statements. I do.

- It feels so good and important for you to be the giver in almost every relationship.
- You feel guilty when someone gives something to you.
- You put the needs of others before your own.
- You avoid or are uncomfortable at the thought of asking for something.[4]

Constant, extravagant giving sounds wonderful, actually biblical, doesn't it? After all, Jesus gave everything He had for us, and He wants us to follow in His footsteps.

But the generosity Jesus displayed came from His heart of love as the Son of God, holy and perfect. We certainly cannot make that claim about ourselves! And when we look at Jesus's life, He clearly did not exhibit a desire to buy followers or friendship. He loved much so He lived generously.

As we seek to live generously and build healthy friendships, we must remember our humanness and our own limits.

Sometimes we introverts can slip easily into a give-all-the-time role. Because we listen well, we see need. And our creative minds love to find ways to meet those needs. But if we return to the idea of living openhanded, that means we must not hug our own need to ourselves, hiding it from others. We must let others step into our pain and need and then cheerfully and gratefully accept their generous offers of help.

We can't do it all for anyone, and we shouldn't try.

Look Honestly at the Motive for Generosity

Have you ever found yourself at a drive-through window hearing the words, "The person ahead of you just paid for your meal"?

I haven't, but I have always wondered what it would feel like to play a part in a pay-it-forward drama. When I found a ten-dollar bill lying in a rain-soaked parking lot one blustery fall morning, I knew I had found my opportunity. Ah! I plotted my strategy. Actually, I crowdsourced ideas on Facebook first and got some great suggestions, including paying someone's layaway bill, buying someone a cup of coffee, giving ten people a dollar each for their favorite charities, and buying protein for a local homeless shelter.[5] All great ideas. I pondered them. I so wanted my moment of "paying it forward" to feel perfect, heartwarming. (I watched the movie.)

For several days I crafted my plan, compiling my crowdsourced ideas. I landed on this: I would go to a local grocery store and find a parent with kids in tow and hand him or her the now-dry ten-dollar bill.

On my self-designated pay-it-forward day, I could hardly wait to get to the grocery store. And when I arrived, I began my research. I looked at other shoppers and imagined how they could use ten dollars. I smiled to myself.

And then, on my second loop around the store, I started feeling a bit sick to my stomach. I realized that my attempt at generosity involved looking for someone "less fortunate," someone needy. And how could I, at a quick glance, in a crowded grocery store, make that assessment? I began to realize that I could actually deeply insult someone by offering a ten-dollar bill. I could make someone wonder, *do I look THAT needy?*

Generosity

Why did I think I could decide who needed my found ten dollars? Why did I think I could look at someone and know his or her story and need?

I almost wished I hadn't discovered that wet ten-dollar bill.

Generosity can get all mixed up with interesting motivations, can't it? I ask a friend a question because I really want him to ask me that same question. I send a gift to a friend on her birthday because I really want her to notice me and give me a gift on my birthday. I bring a gift to the friends who invited me for dinner because the etiquette divas tell me I should. I volunteer my time at the local school because every parent does that, right?

I finally took my ten-dollar bill with me to the cash register and handed it to the clerk at the end of our transaction. "I found this in a parking lot. It isn't mine. Could you use it for the next person's groceries?"

Then I went to bag my own groceries, hoping to slip out of the store quickly.

Within seconds, I heard the cashier say, "That woman over there gave me this ten-dollar bill and said to pass it on to you."

I tried to hide. I had hoped to act as an anonymous donor, but I didn't tell the cashier that. How embarrassing!

And then I heard a soft voice next to me: "Thank you! I so needed that. I'm moving out of my house of thirty years today, and I'm just having a hard day."

As I drove home, I remembered how I had imagined my pay-it-forward experience as I swooped in to offer a rescue to a shopper as if to say, *You look like you need help, so I will step in.* Eek! I'm so glad I didn't insult someone by doing that.

It seems so important as we pursue building friendships through generosity that we routinely spend time asking ourselves *why* we do the generous things we do for friends. Are we trying to mount a rescue? Or manipulate? Or buy a relationship? Or do we seek to communicate one simple message: "I see. I care"?

Jump-Start Friendship with Generosity Practices

How then can we practice genuine, gracious generosity that helps build strong, life-giving friendships without becoming overgivers or people who always feel they need to DO more? And how can we introverts learn to practice generosity in a way that works well for our specific, quiet personality? Beyond sharing our money and possessions with others, how can we cultivate a generous spirit? Consider these six suggestions.

Determine to be generous with your time.

Do you have a coworker who has a car in the shop? Could you offer rides until the car gets fixed? This one-on-one gift of time works so much better for an introvert than volunteering with a friend at a loud, busy Christmas event.

Do you have a neighbor who mentions that she just can't get her paperwork organized (something you love to do)? Could you offer to help her set up a system?

Any generous gifts of time could act as a bridge and an opportunity for a friendship to sprout, even making an Ethiopian casserole. My writer-friend Carlene Hill Byron explains:

Generosity

While serving with the Salvation Army in North Carolina, I worked with Teddy, a man of Ethiopian heritage whose wife, Ariam, had grown up in Eritrea. When Ariam delivered their first child, I wanted to bring the family a meal, but I didn't know what kind of food they might like.

Thanks to the miracle of the internet, I found a recipe for an Ethiopian casserole called Doro Wat. The recipe stretched my international spice collection to its full extent—whole coriander seeds, cumin seeds, dried red chili peppers, whole allspice, whole cloves, black peppercorns, cardamom seeds, paprika, cinnamon, ginger, turmeric, nutmeg, and salt. Finding fenugreek seeds required a bit of shopping, but the little international markets near my house didn't fail me.

I minced onions, sautéed them until golden brown, and then added garlic and sautéed some more. Next, I added the spice mix (which I had already toasted in a dry skillet) and sautéed another thirty minutes. Then I dropped in chicken pieces, and while they cooked (which took another three-quarters of an hour or so), I boiled some eggs in a second pan. I peeled the eggs and dropped them into the sauce with the chicken, so the flavor would penetrate the white—another fifteen minutes.

So after about three hours of cooking, I had a casserole. I transferred it to a plastic covered dish and took it to Teddy and Ariam in the hospital.

Teddy opened the lid and his face lit up. "Look!" he said to Ariam. "She made us Doro Wat!"

I didn't know until then that Doro Wat is a festival dish in Ethiopia. It's the meal you make for New Year's Day. With the egg and the chicken together, it symbolizes the entire circle of life. Pretty perfect for a couple celebrating their first child.

Over the rest of that day, Teddy and Ariam opened the container many times to show Ethiopian friends that their American friend had made them Doro Wat. I'm not sure they ate any, but the meal fed our friendship.[6]

Determine to build up others with words of praise.

Most of us probably associate the word *generosity* with giving money, but how often do we think of practicing generosity with words?

Perhaps you remember as a child hearing a parent say, *I love you* or *I'm proud of you* or *You really seem to enjoy _____* or *I noticed how you used kind words to build up your friend*. Maybe those encouraging words came to you from a teacher or a coach or an extended family member. Those simple words have such power, don't they? Just letters in the alphabet formed into sentences, and yet they can change the course of a life.

My husband told me this story, based on his decades-long experience as an adjunct professor of public speaking.

> This class requires students to confront what surveys consistently reveal to be our greatest fear. It's essential I find ways to affirm novice speakers so they are encouraged to spend a lifetime crafting this skill rather than retiring from it the minute the semester ends.
>
> In my early years, that praise was delivered in one-to-one grading or individual meetings. In a recent class, I added something. After each student had given a speech, I went around the room and publicly offered targeted praise to each student—something specific each speaker had done in his or her presentation that the rest of us could learn from.
>
> Students later contacted me to tell me how much that inspired them—not just that I had praised them, but that I had done it in front of others.
>
> Generous words stated sincerely, intentionally, and sometimes publicly, have an enormous impact on the people in our lives.[7]

Nowhere do words appear more publicly than on social media. In a matter of seconds, we can easily broadcast our words to the world. We think it; we post it. We tell people how we feel, how we think, how we voted, what we had for dinner, and all about our latest achievements.

What would happen, I wonder, if we used our words on social media primarily to praise publicly and encourage others? *Look what my friend did!* or *So happy for you. Yahoo!* or *Grateful for your unique, thoughtful insight on this subject.* And what might happen if we opted for NOT using inflammatory or competitive language on social media?

Honestly, do you find yourself drawn to someone in the workplace who speaks constantly and loudly about himself? More than likely, you find yourself gravitating toward the thoughtful coworker who said, "Congrats on that project. I really like your vision."

We introverts tend to have a deep affection for words. They loll around in our brains continually, but sometimes we have trouble getting them from our brains to our lips in a timely manner. I call it brain freeze.

Introverts often say they prefer communicating via social media rather than in person because it gives them space and time to respond with thoughtfully prepared words, thus avoiding brain freeze. Of course, we cannot do all our connecting online (even in a season of social distancing and shelter-at-home), but for an introvert who wants to connect with others, social media can be a good place to start reaching for people, especially when that connection features generous words of praise for others.

If we want to grow strong, life-giving friendships, we need to develop our repertoire of encouraging words, on and off social media.

> **Introvert Inclinations**
> Truly hear other people's needs after taking time to listen well.
> Rely on written words to communicate precisely.
> Like a slow and steady pace for building friendships.

Determine to believe the best about others.

We can hold grudges and feel slighted so easily: *My neighbor didn't invite me to the party last night. Why don't people respond to my emails and text messages? Why doesn't my friend reciprocate my efforts at getting together?*

So many times we clench our fists around these slights, real or perceived, and we allow ourselves to play the "poor me" loop over and over in our heads. If we value building honest, life-giving friendships, however, we must learn to live "openhandedly" and let go of these slights and assume the best in people.

Instead of thinking, *My friend doesn't reciprocate my effort to get together. She must think I'm not worth her time,* we can (and should) learn to tell ourselves, *I can't know the whole story. I can't guess at her motives. What I can do is make sure that I respond well.*

In her book *Never Unfriended,* Lisa-Jo Baker says it this way:

> Guilt-free friendship says that anytime you get back to me is a good time. Guilt-free friendship says that I will always assume the best about your motivations. Guilt-free friendship says that I won't keep score when it comes to e-mails answered or phone calls returned. Guilt-free friendship focuses on the friendship and ditches the guilt. Guilt-free friendship loves any chance and any slice of time to catch

up; it isn't about criticizing how much or how frequently that happens. Instead, guilt-free friendship is generous and forgiving and creates easy space for reconnecting because it doesn't have any conditions for how or when or how often that happens.[8]

Assuming the best, living openhandedly (letting go of slights), and pursuing guilt-free friendship will take effort. But it will also set us free from ruminating. Not even cows look pretty when they continually chew their cuds. And we introverts, because we spend so much time in our heads, can easily get into a mental loop of chewing on friendship wounds.

Determine to offer the gift of space.

In my first book, *Storm Sisters*, I wrote a lot about my longtime friend, Michelle, and the life storms we have endured together. How I treasure her friendship! These days Michelle has a full-time job, a busy husband, two healthy teenage kids, and (surprise!) other friends. I can't just pop over to her house for a quick cup of coffee while I'm running errands. But I can text her. Or email her. And we've discovered that we can sometimes do a spur-of-the-moment, quick lunch.

On one of those quick lunch days, Michelle hopped in my car and said, "I feel like I should introduce myself." I laughed and nodded. We hadn't seen each other or had a long conversation in weeks. But I truly wasn't seething inside or feeling as if she had let me down. I know how busy her life is. And I completely support her efforts to parent and contribute at her job and grow a strong marriage. Our decades-long friendship can survive this season; it has survived many other seasons.

After that lunch, on the way back to her office, Michelle said, "Thank you for giving me space. At this stage in my life, I just don't have a lot of time."

Her comment made me think. So often we want a best friend who can always listen, always encourage, always support. We expect too much, especially in terms of time. And, truthfully, we can so easily try to control or guilt another person so that we get what we want just the way we want it. That attitude and that behavior do not build a strong, life-giving friendship.

Introverts, in particular, thrive with extra space and time. We need time to think and process and sometimes to stare at the wall to refuel. An extrovert who pushes an introverted friend to engage constantly will stress out that friend and not get him or her at their best.

Let us give each other the gift of space, whether due to circumstances or personality.

Learn to accept graciously another's generous gift.

We cannot assume that if we want friends, we just have to do more, give more. We must also learn to accept the gracious gifts others offer us.

As part of my teacher training in college, our professors did a mock interview. And I still remember one of the questions I received: "What would you do if someone handed you a quarter?"

I answered simply, "I would say thank you."

For weeks after that mock interview, I questioned my answer.

Maybe I should have said, "Oh no. You keep it. I'm sure you need it more than I do."

Maybe I should have said, "This isn't mine. I can't keep it."

Maybe I should have said, "Wow! Really?! You are giving this quarter to me? Lowly me? Poor, college-student me?"

Maybe I should have mentioned that I would find something to give the person in return for the quarter.

When someone gives you something, do you feel awkward? Do you try to refuse the gift? Or make an elaborate, effusive fuss about it? Or think immediately, *What can I give this person tomorrow?*

Building friendships based on generosity depends as much on giving as on receiving. Doing more, giving more, won't build lasting friendships. And we can't know the joy of receiving just what we need from a friend if we have never let that person into our lives enough to see our struggles.

> **Introvert Impediments**
> Easily lose their own, quiet voice in the presence of a louder, needy voice.
> Can focus so much on their own internal life and then forget to pay attention to the external world of others.
> Become overwhelmed and fatigued by a fast-paced, intense friendship.

Gift Yourself with Self-Care

During the COVID-19 crisis, I heard from many introverts some version of what I felt myself: "All of a sudden I have a house full of people, and I'm having trouble finding a quiet spot for myself."

How selfish to want quiet in the days of a worldwide crisis, right? Or not.

My introverted self operates so much better when I have a daily dose of quiet (my fuel). In times of stress and emotional ups and downs, I need that fuel more than ever. When my tank registers full, or at least half-full, I have more patience, kindness, and flexibility.

I really like the way my writing friend April Yamasaki wrestles with the idea of self-care in her book, *Four Gifts*.

> Given this larger landscape of self-care, and given the core commitments that shape our lives, I understand healthy self-care as "me too" rather than "me first" or "me not at all." So to begin, I find it most helpful to consider several questions: What are my core commitments, and how might they shape my self-care? How do I practice self-care—not always first, but in a way that is life-giving and sustaining for me and also allows me to honor my core commitments? Using the framework of Jesus' great commandment, how do I love God, love my neighbor, and still take care of myself?

She explains how this plays out in practical life:

> When parents set aside their own need for sleep to care for a sick child in the middle of the night, in that moment the child's need comes first. For the parent, self-care might be an afternoon nap when the child finally settles down, or time for a walk the next day. In this way, self-care that honors core commitments might be delayed or postponed or after the fact, but it's still self-care even if it sometimes seems to come in second.[9]

During our stay-at-home period when the extroverts in my life wanted to chat or FaceTime or do a Zoom call. I tried to say yes, but I also gave myself permission to say, "I love you, but I just need some time and space of my own. Could we talk later at _____?"

Oh, the dance of self-care—an important dance.

Enter into Someone's Story

Practicing generosity, living with open hands and open hearts, means willingly entering into someone else's story and letting people enter into our story.

One of the best illustrations I know of this kind of living comes from the Bible and involves a group of men:

> When Jesus returned to Capernaum several days later, the news spread quickly that he was back home. Soon the house where he was staying was so packed with visitors that there was no more room, even outside the door. While he was preaching God's word to them, four men arrived carrying a paralyzed man on a mat. They couldn't bring him to Jesus because of the crowd, so they dug a hole through the roof above his head. Then they lowered the man on his mat, right down in front of Jesus. (Mark 2:1–4)

Four men spent enough time with their paralyzed friend to hear his deep desire for healing. And that man spoke honestly of his longing.

Four men let go of what they carried in their hands and used their hands instead to pick up a stretcher.

Four men pooled their wisdom and came up with a creative solution to dig a hole in a roof. (If only they had had power tools!)

Four men let their hearts and faith in Jesus lead the way.

> **Challenge Your Introverted Self**
> Find a way in the next few weeks to offer generous words to someone. Don't let yourself depend on written words. Use your voice—in a quiet, thoughtful way, of course!

Practicing generosity, entering into other people's lives, can feel daunting, especially for us introverts who feel quite content at home. But oh, the healing it can bring for us and for others.

I admire these men—all five of them.

I also admire my mother-in-law, a woman with a unique gift, which I'll tell you about in the next chapter.

Journaling Questions

Before you launch into reading the next chapter, Approachability, pause for a few minutes and pull out a pen to answer these questions.

1. How have you experienced generosity in a friendship? What did it do for that relationship?
2. How have you experienced overgenerosity in a friendship? What did it do to your relationship?
3. Describe your go-to method of offering generosity: time, talents, words, possessions, money.
4. How and when do you most struggle to act generously?
5. How does seeing generosity as an openhanded and openhearted gesture challenge or encourage you in learning to incorporate it into your friendships?
6. How do you respond to the story of the five men in Mark 2? How might it nudge you in your relationship-building?

Chapter 3

Approachability

I initiate because I value more connection in my life.
—Shasta Nelson

My mother-in-law has a gift. She can talk to anyone. I once went to an estate sale with my mother-in-law and one of my sisters-in-law. We had just stepped inside the front door when my mother-in-law paused and smiled at another woman also walking in the door. That woman smiled back, and the two began to talk. I wandered off to look at other things throughout the house, particularly some quilts.

When I returned to the front hall, bulky quilt in hand, I found my mother-in-law still standing in the front hall and still talking to the same woman. *Must be a former neighbor*, I thought. *Or a friend of a friend. Maybe the owner of the house?*

No. These two women had never met each other.

I have lost count of the number of times I've watched my mother-in-law (Mudder) strike up a conversation with a stranger. At a store. At a concert. In an elevator. On a walk around the block. My husband and I have taken to calling this ability "doing a Mudder." And we both deeply admire Mudder's ability to exercise what some might call "a gift of gab."

My mother-in-law naturally connects with people, and that connection appears to energize her. Many people would categorize her as an extrovert.

Living Connected

In her best-selling book *Quiet: The Power of Introverts in a World That Can't Stop Talking,* author Susan Cain writes, "Extroverts enjoy the extra bang that comes from activities like meeting new people, skiing slippery slopes, and cranking up the stereo."[1]

But what if you don't "draw energy from any of those sorts of activities"? What if meeting new people requires you to make great effort? What if interacting with people, especially making small talk, utterly wears you out instead of energizing you as it does my mother-in-law?

Truthfully, I would rather stay home and read (or write) a book in my cozy office, *but* I also know I can't make real friends, face-to-face friends, that way. *And* I know that God calls me to connect, to share His love with people.

So how do we introverts learn to practice approachability—friendliness, agreeableness, congeniality, affability[2]—in our own quiet, thoughtful sort of way? We can't make friends unless we exhibit at least some degree of friendliness (approachability).

For a stretch of months during the COVID-19 crisis, our daughter and her tuxedo cat, Soupy Bonjour lived with us and our dog, Ringo, a cockapoo. During that time Annalisa started her job as an RN at an ICU. (Whew!)

Every morning I tried to approach Soupy to rub her head as I did Ringo. She skittered off. Ironically, when I started to ignore her, she then started to approach me by weaving herself in and out of my legs and rubbing her head on my leg.

Ringo, on the other hand, continued standing at the bottom of the stairs every morning, tail wagging with enthusiasm, waiting for a rub on the head between his ears. And then, after a morning walk, he delighted

Approachability

in crawling into my lap for a long nap—a bit awkward when I tried to type on a laptop.

To Ringo, connection meant I touched him, and he touched me. Even if I shoved him off my lap to do some typing on my laptop, he scooched over until his back-end smashed into my leg.

To Soupy, connection meant she wrapped herself around me for a few minutes and then wandered off to stare out the window.

Ringo struggled to know how to connect with Soupy. He tried the usual dog things—sniffing her butt, trying to start a chase around the living room. Soupy responded with a quick left hook and/or a hiss. After several months, Ringo seemed finally to have developed a new technique, at least occasionally. He learned to sidle over to Soupy, look in the opposite direction, and just stand still.

And Soupy discovered that when Ringo curled up like a question mark and slept soundly, she could creep toward him and sniff his butt and give him a good stare.

As I watched this cat/dog drama play out daily, I thought about how we human beings have similar drama. Some of us act like friendly cockapoos: *I just want to meet you and touch you and talk to you and hang out with you and just be with you."* Others of us, maybe a lot of us introverts, act a bit more like a cat: *I want to know you but in small doses and on my own terms and in my own time.*

Who is right? The cat? Or the dog?

Both.

And that's the challenge of building relationships. How can we know when and how to connect with others whose personalities differ greatly from ours? And how do we introverts, learn to practice approachability—friendliness, agreeableness, congeniality, affability—in our own quiet sort of way?

Communicate Approachability Despite Social Distancing

As I wrote this chapter, our world had shifted dramatically. To prove it, we now have a new term in our everyday vocabulary: *social distancing*. Officials all over the world told us daily to keep our distance from one another, preferably six feet. And so, I sat at home and wrote this chapter on building relationships through approachability. What irony!

My introverted self settled easily into this quiet period of social distancing. These peaceful rhythms fueled my soul. I happily spent time with books, music, coffee, and thoughts. And yet my heart ached as I heard about seniors, some critically ill in facilities, who could no longer have any visitors. Or international students who could not return to their families. Or medical workers who lived isolated to protect their loved ones.

In spite of enjoying the solitude, I still reached often for my phone to text or email. I wanted to connect with my people. Were they okay? Did they have enough food and toilet paper? How were they navigating the ever-changing landscape of work and home? Did they still have a job?

We introverts often struggle to talk on the phone and instead gravitate toward texting or emailing. But during the COVID-19 crisis, if we wanted to stay connected to friends and loved ones who don't like or don't have the ability to communicate by email or text, we all had to at least try to talk on the phone.

As the weeks of quarantine wore on, I began to experiment with ways to talk to friends and family: Zoom, FaceTime, Skype, What'sApp . . . I realized that

I felt more comfortable on Zoom or FaceTime rather than just having a phone call with no video.

Why?

Body language.

I could easily see a slumping of the shoulders that could indicate a bit of fatigue or discouragement. I could clearly observe a nodding head, indicating agreement with something I said, or a look of confusion about a comment I made.

Watching someone talk on a screen also helped me discern a comma from a period in conversation. I so don't like interrupting someone mid-thought, but it happens all the time in phone calls.

Practicing approachability, friendliness, in a time of social distancing took effort for all of us, but probably especially for extroverts, like my mother-in-law and my husband, who thrive on in-person encounters. So very hard to communicate thoroughly over Zoom.

> **Introvert Inclinations**
> Believe that a book can become a wonderful, silent companion.
> May have a catlike approach to relationships: *I want to know you but in small doses and on my own terms and in my own time.*
> Find a measure of comfort in social distancing.

Communicate Approachability without Saying Anything

After watching my mother-in-law connect so easily with other people, I realized that I could and should learn from her. I do not want to try to become an extrovert or even learn to pretend to function as one, but I *do* so want to learn how to connect with others in my own quiet, thoughtful way.

Admire and adapt.

That has become my motto as I think and watch and read and pray about connecting as an introvert. What techniques do I admire in others, including extroverts, and how can I adapt those techniques for my quiet soul?

I've begun to learn that I can always lean in to listen well, smile, and nod my head. None of that actually requires me to speak. Perfect for an introvert!

Leaning into a conversation says, *I want to hear your words more clearly. They sound interesting.* Don't we all appreciate someone responding to us with interest?

Several years ago, I also started the rather intimidating practice of making eye contact with others in stores or out on walks. I usually did not talk. Just smiled.

One winter Saturday morning I dashed to a store just before closing time. I walked toward the register to discover a line and one clerk. Ugh!

I smiled at the woman to my right. She smiled back and said, "You go ahead of me. Really, it is fine."

"That is so nice of you! Are you sure?"

"Yes. I'm actually enjoying the wait."

"Really?"

"I am."

"Thank you!" I smiled and continued to stand near her. We made eye contact a few more times and exchanged a few more smiles. I resisted taking my phone out of my pocket. She took a step toward me. And then she started to talk about her recent caregiving responsibilities and her weariness.

Approachability

"I'm enjoying the peace of standing here waiting. I never thought I would say that. And I can't believe I'm telling you all of this."

Apparently, I had communicated approachability. I hadn't said much, but I did make eye contact multiple times. And I resisted the temptation to bury my head in my phone.

As challenging as that encounter felt for my quiet soul, I knew that I had given this woman a gift that morning. I had seen her and heard her. I had reminded her, mostly by listening and smiling, that she mattered.

And that made me smile.

Know When Not to Approach

The moment I just described happened on a lazy Saturday, a day when I did not have a lot of other people interaction. My tank felt full so I could stretch.

But what if my tank had felt empty? What if I had encountered this woman after a twelve-hour day full of conversation and conflict?

A friend told me an honest story that makes me think.

> I attended a conference several years ago. The only person I knew was one of the speakers, so there wasn't any opportunity for us to connect while I was there. I was definitely flying solo. It was kind of easy to do this during workshops and general sessions because we were all focused on the speakers.
>
> But when lunchtime rolled around, I was seriously stressed. It was so bad that I called my sister on the phone, so I had the phone as a buffer. I didn't want anyone to feel the urge to strike up a conversation in the food line because

it would ultimately lead to them wanting to sit with me when all I wanted was some quiet time to eat, relax, think, etc.

Once I found a table—the smallest possible, with only two seats—and got situated, I ended the call with my sister and immediately took out a book or something to give off as many "do not approach" vibes as possible.

I was still on edge though because I've been in plenty of situations where people ignored all the context clues and still invited themselves into my space.[3]

We introverts get easily overwhelmed in a crowd, especially at places like conferences. My friend had a creative solution. Another might include grabbing food and eating outside or in a secluded room.

I have come home sick from way too many conferences and retreats because I have utterly worn myself out connecting. I keep working to learn that I must pace myself in terms of effort spent approaching others. I need at least a semifull tank, fueled by quiet, to initiate or even respond well to an approachability encounter.

Reach across Cultures

Clearly, communicating approachability poses challenges for introverts, but it also comes with challenges when it involves people from different cultures.

When my husband took me to Norway in the early years of our marriage, I felt a bit overwhelmed, especially in the grocery store. I couldn't read the labels. Do they sell decaf coffee? Was that drinkable yogurt in a milk carton? And pudding in a cardboard container? And then what was his grandmother, who spoke only Norwegian, trying to tell me?

Joe Navarro, author of *What Every Body Is Saying*, tells the poignant story of moving to America as a

Approachability

young boy and trying to understand a new language and culture.

> When I was eight years old, I came to America as an exile from Cuba. We left just a few months after the Bay of Pigs invasion, and we honestly thought we would be here only for a short while as refugees.
>
> Unable to speak English at first, I did what thousands of other immigrants coming to this country have done. I quickly learned that to fit in with my new classmates at school, I needed to be aware of—and sensitive to—the "other" language around me, the language of nonverbal behavior. I found that was a language I *could* translate and understand immediately. In my young mind, I saw the human body as a kind of billboard that transmitted (advertised) what a person was thinking via gestures, facial expressions, and physical movements that I could read.[4]

Navigating daily life in a foreign culture stretches everyone. And so does trying to make friends. Just how do we cultivate approachability with people of other cultures and races, especially as an introvert?

Smile! Or not.

A group of students at Brown University decided to get an international perspective on two questions: Why do Americans ask people how they are without waiting for an answer? Why do they smile at complete strangers? Here are a few of the comments they received:

> In **South Korea**, people do not say "hi" or "hello," or even nod to strangers. If you do so, there is a high chance of being ignored.
>
> In **Mexico** we think of Americans as cold or distant but only because in Latin America we are overly

affectionate. We are used to hugging and giving one kiss on the cheek.

Every **Chinese** student wants to make friends and know more about American friends. . . . While it is natural for an American to smile and keep eye contact while talking, it is not natural to me even if I want to be friendly.[5]

Although I have adopted the personal habit of making eye contact and smiling at strangers, I realize that this habit might not work with people of other cultures, and it might not work for every personality type.

I have always loved a particular story in the New Testament (John 4) because it shows Jesus reaching across cultural barriers to connect with a woman. He didn't pay attention to the prevailing cultural winds or even the current religious teachings of Jewish superiority. Instead, he looked this woman (not a Jew) in the eye, maybe smiled, and engaged her in conversation—something the people she encountered on a daily basis seemed reluctant to do.

The story depicts Jesus traveling from Judea north to Galilee. He could have taken several routes, but He chose one that took Him through a country called Samaria, a place the religious leaders of the time avoided. They did not like any association with the Samaritans, a mixed race, who had built their own temple and veered from the standard religious practices of the day.

By noon Jesus had arrived at the village of Sychar, no doubt hot, thirsty, and covered with dust. He approached a well and noticed a woman there. Most of the women in the area went to the well in the morning

Approachability

and again in the evening and no doubt made time to catch up with each other as they drew water for their households. But this woman went to the well at noon. Did she want to avoid gossiping tongues who knew about her multiple divorces? Did she just want some introvert time? Did she hope for invisibility from other townspeople?

At the well Jesus did something religious leaders forbade: He approached a strange woman in public and spoke to her. In fact, he asked her for a drink of water: "The Samaritan woman, taken aback, asked, 'How come you, a Jew, are asking me, a Samaritan woman, for a drink?' (Jews in those days wouldn't be caught dead talking to Samaritans.)" (John 4:9 MSG). The conversation continued, and Jesus gently probed this woman's pain and then offered her healing, calling it "living water": "Jesus answered, 'If you knew the generosity of God and who I am, you would be asking *me* for a drink, and I would give you fresh, living water'" (John 4:10 MSG).

Clearly, Jesus saw this woman, even though she might have wished for invisibility. Jesus did not view her as an irritation to avoid but rather as a woman of value with an aching heart. He saw her, talked to her, and treated her with dignity.

What a great example for us as we seek to connect with others in our culturally diverse world in a quiet, thoughtful sort of way.

If Jesus had obeyed the cultural dictates of His day, this woman would never have heard the good news of the living water.

And that compels and challenges me, even as an introvert, to work at connecting with others despite perceived differences of race and culture. I want to live as Jesus lived and speak His words of healing into other people's lives. I can't do that if I don't learn to practice some measure of approachability—friendliness, agreeableness, congeniality, affability.

Smiling might serve as a good starting point. But what other techniques can we introverts cultivate in an attempt to connect with others in a quiet, thoughtful sort of way?

Notice and Respond to Others' Approachability Cues

My mother-in-law naturally approaches others, but my quiet soul needs a little prompting in order to approach someone. That often comes through nonverbal cues, including eye contact and body language.

My introvert tendencies give me the gift of seeing and noticing and processing. All of that helps me read people. So did a book (of course!).

In his book, *The Dictionary of Body Language,* author Joe Navarro describes more than four hundred of the most important body-language observations he made over his twenty-five-year career in the FBI in the areas of counterintelligence and behavioral assessment. For example, he says, "The slow, intentional rise of a single shoulder, coupled with a head tilt toward the same shoulder while making direct eye contact, signifies a personal interest."[6]

I think I knew that intuitively, but after reading this book, I do certainly pay more attention to the way people stand or use their hands or move their heads.

Obviously, body language can't tell the whole story, but it can help us introverts learn to approach others and signal others that we welcome connection.

Asking ourselves two key questions can also help.

Approachability

What Do I See?

This would include body language cues but could also include a glance at hair and clothes and shoes. Workout clothes could mean, *I'm on my way to the gym. Gotta run. No time to talk.* Hair up in a messy bun accompanied by pajama pants might mean, *I ran to the store hoping I wouldn't see anyone I know. I just want to get in and out of here.* Keys in hand could indicate someone eager to leave, not converse.

What Do I Hear?

Do I hear other people, including little kids, vying for this person's attention? Does this present environment buzz with people and loud music, making any sort of conversation a challenge? If we do start a conversation, do I hear words like "good to see you" or "wish I had more time"?

During the COVID-19 crisis, for the first time in my life, I found myself walking around a grocery store full of people wearing masks. I felt as if I had walked into a sci-fi movie. As I looked at the faces of my fellow shoppers, I longed to see a smile of reassurance, as if to say, *We'll get through this!* It felt so surreal to wander around a store seeing eyes, just eyes. And almost every pair of those eyes squinted. Even I could tell that squinty eyes indicated stress.

When I checked out, I found myself trying to smile with my eyes (hard to do!) at the cashier to say, "Thank you for working today so I could get food." So frustrating not to have a smile to communicate!

But that experience also served as a good reminder that I do have to "use my words" on occasion to communicate approachability. (Chapter 4 has lots of suggestions on how to develop and ask questions.)

Cultivate Approachability on Social Media

So much of our sharing of words happens on social media these days, a place where introverts often feel comfortable because they can participate from the quiet of their own space.

When I first entered the world of social media, I felt bewildered. What to post? Where to post? When to post? Facebook? Twitter? Why? Over and over I heard experts say, "As a writer, you have to build a platform, a place where people can see you and interact with you online." But I didn't (still don't) want to build a platform. I just want to make friends. I want to connect.

I decided to study a few people on Facebook to see what and when they posted. One of my favorites quickly became author Lauraine Snelling. I discovered that she often posts about her chickens, her painting classes, her flowers, or some of the everyday challenges of life, such as an uncooperative computer. Except for the chickens and the painting, her life sounds kind of like mine. I can easily imagine inviting Lauraine over to my backyard for a glimpse of my perennials and a cup of tea. Turns out that Lauraine Snelling also happens to be a best-selling author of more than eighty books and has sold more than 5 million copies of those books. But that does not appear splashed daily all over her online presence. Instead, she communicates approachability by showing readers glimpses of her real life all mixed up with her writing life.[7]

What might happen on social media if we reclaimed it as a place to connect, to build bridges, instead of a place to vent? What if every time we posted, we asked ourselves one simple question: *How will this post help me build a bridge to another person?*

Approachability

Many people form a first impression based on social media. Does our social media say, *I'm approachable, friendly*? Or does it say, *I have strong opinions*?

Foster Approachability by Admitting Mistakes

Part of cultivating approachability online or in person involves admitting our imperfections. Not easy to do.

This letter from President Abraham Lincoln to General Ulysses S. Grant speaks volumes:

> I do not remember that you and I ever met personally. I write this now as a grateful acknowledgment for the almost inestimable service you have done the country. I wish to say a word further. When you first reached the vicinity of Vicksburg, I thought you should do, what you finally did—march the troops across the neck, run the batteries with the transports, and thus go below; and I never had any faith, except a general hope that you knew better than I, that the Yazoo Pass expedition, and the like, could succeed. When you got below, and took Port Gibson, Grand Gulf, and vicinity, I thought you should go down the river and join Gen. Banks; and when you turned Northward East of the Big Black, I feared it was a mistake. I now wish to make the personal acknowledgment that you were right, and I was wrong.[8]

We all make mistakes. How we react after we make one can either open a door for connecting to others or add another brick to a wall that keeps us at a distance from others.

May we learn to embrace that phrase, "You were right. I was wrong."

> **Introvert Impediments**
> Struggle to initiate times of connection.
> Feel easily intimidated in a crowd of unknown people at a social event.
> Don't always feel comfortable making eye contact with strangers.

Become an Initiator

We all like to feel noticed and appreciated and feel flattered when we receive an invitation to a meal or an event.

But this just doesn't happen a lot.

The reality of trying to build a strong, life-giving friendship often means that, at least at the beginning, one person does a lot of the initiating. Someone has to. We can't all just sit in our homes or apartments and assume someone will wander over, knock on the door, and want to strike up a conversation and then eventually want to cultivate a friendship.

We have to make effort. We have to become initiators. We have to remember the motivating story of Jesus at the well. May we have His eyes to see and His ears to hear. Even us introverts.

In her thoughtful book about friendships (*Friendtimacy*), author Shasta Nelson offers this Initiator Mantra:

> I am the primary initiator in my relationships—not because there is something wrong with me, but because there is something right with me. I initiate because I value more connection in my life. I initiate because a relationship requires it in order to get any momentum, and I can give that gift. I initiate because this world needs more people who prioritize relationships, and I'm willing to be one of them. I initiate because I'm the one who *knows* the benefit of more connection. I initiate because I am brave, because I value love, and because I am ready for more.[9]

Approachability

We can so easily keep score in relationships: *I called her last week. Why isn't she calling me this week?* or *I've traveled to see my friend every year for the past ten years, but he has only come to see me once.*

We want all things equal in relationships, especially in terms of effort, don't we? What if we stopped keeping score and simply adopted Shasta's Initiator Mantra or developed a simple Introverted Initiator Mantra of our own, such as, *I will initiate one connection every week (or month) with a friend or a potential friend?*

These words from *The Message* say it so well: "Here is a simple, rule-of-thumb guide for behavior: Ask yourself what you want people to do for you, then grab the initiative and do it for them" (Matthew 7:12).

Imagine a world where we all worked hard to approach others, to initiate in relationships—a world where more of us, even introverts, felt connected and heard rather than alone and angry.

> **Challenge Your Introverted Self**
> Come up with a plan for connecting with a stranger in the next month or so. Imagine the scenario in your head. Where will it most likely happen? What will you do? Do you need to speak? If so, what might you say?

We introverts can't expect, or even try, to turn into extroverts like my mother-in-law. But we can admire and adapt their techniques to fit our own quiet and thoughtful personalities by finding creative ways to present an air of approachability, friendliness. Eye contact, verbal cues, and body language certainly help, but so does cultivating a sense of curiosity and an ability to ask open-ended questions—something we'll discuss in the next chapter.

Journaling Questions

Before your curiosity makes you turn the page and head for the next chapter, take a few minutes and work through these questions that will help you personalize what you're reading and learning.

1. How easily do you approach people you don't know? What motivates you or holds you back?
2. Pay attention to body language during your next face-to-face interaction with someone. What did you notice about the other person's body language? What did you notice about your own body language? How did body language cues help you connect?
3. When you read the story of Jesus and the woman at the well (John 4), what stands out? How does this story challenge you as an introvert?
4. If you have a presence on social media, what words would an impartial observer use to describe it? What words would you like people to use to describe your social media presence?
5. What approachability technique can you adopt as you seek to connect with others in a quiet, thoughtful sort of way?
6. Write your own version of an Introverts Initiator Mantra.

Chapter 4

Curiosity

After all, there's nothing in the world as interesting as people, and one is never done with studying them.
—Vincent Van Gogh

Willow intrigued me. When she made a comment in our small group Bible study, I could tell that she had done the lesson thoroughly and taken the time to let it seep into her daily life. I loved the sound of her bubbling-over laugh at the telling of some quirky story. And when she mentioned a family struggle in a few succinct words during our prayer time, I noticed how easily the tears slipped from her eyes.

When Willow frequently took a turn to lead our group, I marveled. I knew that she, like me, claimed the title of introvert. I knew that in order to prepare and lead our group, she had invested a tremendous amount of personal energy and conquered a chorus of screaming, internal self-doubters.

I learned so much from her, and I also realized that I wanted to know more about Willow. What fueled her? What challenged her? What experiences had created such depth within her? I sensed that thousands of conversations would never truly mine the depths of Willow.

My curiosity compelled me to initiate a connection with her outside our normal group meeting.

Living Connected

We emailed a bit, and I discovered from Facebook that Willow loves to garden, do crafts, and cook.

One day, years after I had stopped attending the Bible study, I asked Willow if she would like to have lunch with me after her leader's meeting. We met at a little restaurant down the hill and had a delightful conversation, punctuated with laughter.

And then Willow invited me out to her house to see her garden, something we had discussed over lunch. As I stepped into her backyard, full of raised beds brimming with flowers and vegetables, I asked lots of questions: What is this plant? Does it need full sun? How do you cook with this vegetable? Why do you cover your blueberries with netting?

Over lunch in her sun-filled kitchen, I asked more questions about her favorite recipes.

Like most introverts, Willow took the time to form the answers to my questions in her head before she spoke. We did not have a rapid-fire conversation, and I loved that! I find great joy and energy in quiet, deliberate conversations.

How glad I am that curiosity, something we introverts typically have in abundance, compelled me to reach out to Willow and granted me in return the gift of friendship.

Brian Grazer, a Hollywood movie producer of *Apollo 13*, *A Beautiful Mind*, the television show *24*, and many other titles, put a name to this habit of interacting with people by asking questions. In his book, *A Curious Mind*, he explains how at the age of twenty-three, he decided to develop a lifelong practice he calls "Curiosity Conversations." He asks for a one-hour meeting with someone and then asks that person questions. His goal? "I want to understand what makes people tick; I want to see if I can connect a person's attitude and personality with their work, with their challenges and accomplishments."[1]

Over the years Grazer has met with men and women from all walks of life, including Isaac Asimov, Mark Cuban, Jim Lovell, Condoleezza Rice, Oprah Winfrey, and Princess Diana.

He doesn't ask for a job or push a movie idea. He simply asks questions and listens, wanting to learn more about each interesting person.

How, I wonder, would our relationships grow, if we, like Brian Grazer, let curiosity lead the way?

Did Curiosity Really Kill the Cat?

As I watched our children learn to walk and talk, I marveled at all they learned in just a few short years. I particularly loved watching them find language for the things they saw and the ideas they thought.

Our son, Karl, loved to ask questions as a toddler: "Why is the sky blue? Why is the grass green?" Back then, I couldn't just Google it or ask Siri or Alexa. We did frequently pull out a gold-edged volume of *The World Book Encyclopedia* from the set that my grandparents had given us. Even then, I often said to our curious son, "That is a really good question. I don't know the answer." He remains curious today, including figuring out how to fix engines, stoves, and air conditioners with a little help from YouTube.

Perhaps you remember your own curiosity as a child. *Why does that machine work that way? Why does that plant smell so bad? Why does that person always seem to make me mad?*

Maybe you also remember a parent, grandparent, or teacher saying "Curiosity killed the cat" as a way to warn you, with a touch of humor, to step away from the hot stove or not to try cooking a random mix of chemicals over a Bunsen burner in chemistry lab.

This phrase seems to have mutated from an earlier phrase, "Care killed the cat," used by Shakespeare. In *Much Ado About Nothing*, Claudio says, "What, courage, man! What though care killed a cat, thou hast mettle enough in thee to kill care."[2]

Somehow, over centuries that original phrase about care (worry, concern) morphed into a negative portrayal of curiosity, something dangerous even.[3] Hmm...

Why, I wonder, did someone feel the need to classify curiosity as dangerous enough to kill a cat?

And why, by the time many of us reach adulthood, have we stopped asking *why* and *how*? We focus instead on the facts. We create to-do lists with myriad details to which we must attend. We no longer allow ourselves the time to sit and think and wonder.

I remember memorizing lists of facts for history classes in high school and college, facts that left my head minutes after the test. I wonder if I might have remembered more about history had I focused on the *why* and *how*.

Perhaps curiosity didn't kill the cat but rather "studying for the test" or checking off items on a to-do list actually killed curiosity.

Curiosity. A desire to know. Wondering about the *why* and *how*, and even *what if* of our world and the people in it.

We introverts, who live in our heads surrounded by ideas and words, often have a great affinity for the concept of *curiosity*. We like thinking about *why* and *how* and *what if*. We can't seem to help ourselves.

So what if we could harness this powerful curiosity and then let it loose within our relationships? What

Curiosity

if we could recapture some of the curiosity we had as children? What if instead of curiosity killing the cat or to-do lists killing curiosity, curiosity breathed new life into relationships?

> **Introvert Inclinations**
> Have a natural affinity for curiosity and the questions *why, how,* and *what if.*
> Feel at home in the world of ideas.
> Love to learn from books.

Why Do We Fear Curiosity?

A friend told me this story about curiosity.

> About four years ago I was at a party for people from a meetup group I had been attending for several months. People were mingling with drinks and appetizers, and I was happily talking to people I knew. At one point I went back to the kitchen and a guy was there leaning on the counter not talking to anyone. I had never seen him at any of the meetups, so I was curious about him. He looked to be about twenty years younger than me and probably a body-builder (um, let's just say *I'm not*). My first instinct was not to say anything, but curiosity won out and I asked him, "I haven't seen you before–what's your connection to this thing?"
>
> He had a really nice smile, I think we both found it easy to talk, and the conversation took off. Eventually, I heard the incredible story of how he had been totally immersed in the fundamentalist religion of his parents until in his late twenties he started having doubts about the veracity of it (aka, curiosity). By age thirty-three, he no longer believed any of it and could not keep up the pretense. He decided to tell his parents, knowing what they would have to do. And they did it: they disowned him, their only child. That was a year prior to the night we were talking, and he had not had any contact from them or with.[4]

How sad that curiosity trumped relationship when it could so easily have enhanced it.

Many people quote St. Augustine as saying, "God fashioned hell for the inquisitive."[5]

When I hunted through Augustine's *Confessions* to verify this quotation, however, I found something much different (bold emphasis mine).

> How, then, shall I respond to him who asks, "What was God doing *before* he made heaven and earth?" I do not answer, as a certain one is reported to have done facetiously (shrugging off the force of the question). "He was preparing hell," he said, "for those who pry too deep." It is one thing to see the answer; it is another to laugh at the questioner—and for myself I do not answer these things thus. More willingly would I have answered, *"I do not know what I do not know,"* than cause one who asked a deep question to be ridiculed—and by such tactics gain praise for a worthless answer.[6]

I see here Augustine's respect for the person who asks the deep question. Not disdain.

How, I wonder, might our relationships change or even improve if we made room for deep questions? What if we learned to say some version of, *"That is a really good question?"* What if we learned to say, "I don't know the answer" rather than quickly offering our opinion as a definitive answer.

Especially when we speak of faith, could we invite rather than dismiss curiosity into the conversation? Instead of fearing curiosity, could we embrace it?

Consider this scenario. Which answer opens the door to further conversation and functions as an invitation to relationship?

Curiosity

Q: Why would God allow all the suffering in this world?
A: We just have to trust God.

versus

A: Really good question! I've had it myself. I don't know the answer. The writer of the Book of Job in the Bible had the same questions.

Throughout the New Testament, we read about the many interactions Jesus had with people and the many questions He asked. In Mark 8:27-29 we read:

> Jesus and his disciples left Galilee and went up to the villages near Caesarea Philippi. As they were walking along, he asked them, "Who do people say I am?"
>
> "Well," they replied, "some say John the Baptist, some say Elijah, and others say you are one of the other prophets."
>
> Then he asked them, "But who do you say I am?"

Over and over again in His interactions with people, Jesus asked questions meant to make listeners think and own what they believed.

- "You are the salt of the earth. But what good is salt if it has lost its flavor? Can you make it salty again?" (Matthew 5:13)
- "Can all your worries add a single moment to your life?" (Matthew 6:27)
- "And why worry about a speck in your friend's eye when you have a log in your own?" (Matthew 7:3)

A deep question forces us to think, to probe, and we introverts have brains just oozing with deep questions. These questions can create fear and a sense of instability for a time, but ultimately, they should also promote growth and change. And growth and change lead the way for developing new friendships and deepening acquaintance-type relationships into friendships.

Do Curious People Really Have Better Relationships?

I loved reading to my children as they grew, including some favorites such as the *Curious George* series. Amazing what a little monkey can think to do!

I recently checked out a stack of *Curious George* books so I could reread these yellow-covered classics all about curiosity. As I read, and laughed, I kept noticing how curiosity got George into a lot of trouble and caused lots of frustration for his friend, the man with the big yellow hat.

In *Curious George Takes a Job,* George's curiosity takes him on a meander through his city where he discovers spaghetti, gets a job as a window washer, paints someone's apartment with safari animals, and eventually breaks his leg jumping from a fire escape. The story makes the newspaper and (spoiler alert) eventually reunites George with the man with the big yellow hat.

The story ends with this line: "He was a good little monkey—he had only one fault: he was too curious."[7]

Ouch! Curiosity doesn't fare too well in this tale. Perhaps the author had in mind that phrase, "Curiosity killed the cat."

Is curiosity really a fault?

George Mason University psychology professor Todd B. Kashdan begs to differ. His clinical research

Curiosity

has led him to state, "Being interested is more important in cultivating a relationship and maintaining a relationship than being interesting; that's what gets the dialogue going. . . . It's the secret juice of relationships."[8]

In his book, *Curious? Discover the Missing Ingredient to a Fulfilling Life,* Dr. Kashdan describes one of the research studies he conducted that led him to this conclusion.

> Strangers were brought into our lab to spend five minutes getting acquainted. Before these interactions, participants filled out questionnaires so we could rank them in order from least to most curious. What we found was that the more curious a person was, the more they enjoyed interacting with strangers and the closer they felt to them by the end. But the positive experience wasn't just "in their heads." The partners of the most curious people felt the same way, too.
>
> In looking for the traits that led to these beneficial exchanges, we found that curious people treat their partners as vast unknown territories to be explored, asking lots of questions, as they continually penetrate deeper into new terrain. The people who talked to very curious people appeared to enjoy being in the spotlight of this undivided attention.
>
> It feels good when someone is interested in you. It makes you feel desirable, causing you to be more interested in and feel close to the person showering attention on you.[9]

Our friend Falecia would agree with Kashdan. She has watched this principle play over and over again in her time abroad. A third-generation Samoan-Mexican-American, who grew up in California, Falecia now lives in Granada, Spain, where she serves with a local church and pursues a master's degree in theology.

Living Connected

I met Jesús in Sevilla in the fall of 2017 as part of my study abroad *intercambio* program (a cultural exchange in which an American practices their Spanish and a Spaniard practices their English). We were randomly assigned as partners.

My first impression of him made me think we wouldn't get along. He said some things I didn't understand or agree with.

But I like to give people multiple chances. I know myself. It takes me a while to open up to people. A lot of people have said to me, "At first I thought you were really serious, but then I realized you were more laid back."

I'm glad I did. He's one of the funniest people I know. We've been best friends since!

Curiosity fosters this friendship because we're constantly asking questions about the other's perspective, culture, etc.—"Why do Spaniards do this? Is America really like in the movies?"

And I've been challenged to learn more about my Samoan heritage because it's an aspect of my personality/character that Jesús really notices (compared to other American friends of his) and that's sparked/revived a curiosity in me that's always been there but that I haven't dedicated time to because of life's circumstances.

We speak in Spanish. One day he asked me if he could practice his English with me for an exam. Halfway through we had to switch to Spanish.

We said to each other, "I don't even know who you are when you don't speak Spanish!" We had gotten used to the sound of each other's voice in Spanish. Personality may not come through in language. Jesús speaks very quickly and emotively in Spanish. He tries in English but doesn't come across the same way.

Any friendships, especially a cross-cultural one, benefits from a clearing of the air, getting to a point where you can say, "Did you mean this? I don't understand." No need to feel dumb about clarifying.

Curiosity

> I've discovered that it is fun to ask questions to get further clarification. It has led to some good laughs, including the time I tried to explain the term *pickup line*.[10]

Curiosity may get cats, monkeys, and people into trouble, but clearly it can also foster friendships, especially when it leads us to ask thoughtful questions.

Got Questions?

Falecia, like all curious people I know, loves to ask questions. They can't help themselves.

My husband, John, also loves questions and often talks about his first jobs in radio and how they taught him to ask questions.

> In my first radio job just out of college, I mostly went to news conferences. A lot of television, radio, and print journalists were there since the station was in the state capital. I was shy and intimidated. Typically, I stayed quiet and deferred to the older, more experienced reporters. I sort of got away with it since there were plenty of other people asking questions, and I could use the answers those questions generated to submit to my station. But then two years later I got my second radio job, and the next thing I knew I was hosting a weekday interview show. Now I didn't have a roomful of reporters carrying me. It was just the guest and me. I had no choice but to ask questions—and a lot of them—to fill the time.
>
> It took me a while, but I got into a rhythm in this new work assignment. I learned that people like to be given the chance to talk about things interesting to them and that they found my curiosity winsome.
>
> Asking questions naturally started happening not just in my radio job but also in my personal life. I would meet someone new and kind of flip into reporter mode. I learned to come up quickly with a couple of questions. I learned not

to be afraid to ask a stupid question. I also learned to enjoy taking on the role of someone who knows nothing talking to someone who knows everything. I discovered that people like being treated as experts in their area and that they give me a lot of grace as I stumble my way toward learning.

I love to start a sentence with, "Let me ask you this . . ." It basically communicates: "You are the center of attention right now, and I am interested in what interests you."

I am not sure where I heard this, but a phrase that sticks with me is: "We're all ignorant, just about different things." So whether it's my neighbor who is a pilot, a college student who is studying some subject I can't pronounce, or a stranger at a block party with a hobby I have never heard of, they all have something unique to say.

By asking questions, I learn a lot and along the way build lasting connections and friendships.[11]

Not everyone has John's honed question-asking skills. I don't. In fact, as an introvert, I often get tongue-tied when I meet new people. My brain sort of freezes. So, I have learned to have a few questions in my head when I meet new people.

At a block party, I might ask:

- When did you move into the neighborhood?
- How is living here different for you than where you used to live?
- How do you feel about pizza? We have a great pizza place down the hill.

At a conference with people I don't know well, I might ask:

- How did you hear about this conference?
- What made you decide to come?
- Who else do you know here?

Curiosity

At a wedding reception where I'm seated next to people I've never met, I might ask:

- What is your connection to the bride and groom?
- How far did you have to travel to get here?
- What was your favorite part of the ceremony?

Author Adam McHugh makes an interesting point about questions: "A lot of people are good at asking the first question. However, it's the *second* question that often unlocks the conversation. . . . It is deceivingly simple, but I know of no better second question than, 'Can you tell me more about that?'"[12]

Many years ago, we started a practice of keeping a wooden box filled with questions written on little strips of paper on our dining room table. John loves to "collide worlds" and invite people to dinner who don't know each other well. To help facilitate people getting to know each other, we often pass the box around the table and ask guests to pull out a question and answer it. Sometimes everyone demands to answer each question. We often end up laughing, sometimes feel moved to tears, but always we know more about our guests than we did when they first sat down at our table. And often people who came as strangers leave as friends. Our box includes the following questions:

- What was a really happy time in your life.?
- If you could have witnessed anything in the Bible, what would you have wanted to see?
- How have your priorities changed over time?
- If you could go to the airport right now and get on any flight, where would you go?
- What skill do you wish you had? Why?

- If you could travel back in time, what year would you visit? Why?

As an introvert, I love this question-asking sort of dinner party. It keeps the loudest voice from dominating, and it allows the quiet voices time to emerge. It provides focus. It helps us communicate on a level deeper than talking about jobs and family.

We introverts don't thrive in small-talk situations. In fact, lots of introverts simply refuse to attend events that require small talk: *I don't do small talk.* But my love of Jesus compels me to connect and thus to show up at events that matter to my people. I find it so much easier to show up if I bring my curiosity with me in the form of a few preplanned questions.

> **Introvert Impediments**
> Struggle to think of relevant questions on their feet.
> Prefer not to interrupt someone so they often don't manage to make their quiet voice (or question) heard.
> Don't like conflict, so may avoid asking questions that could cause conflict.

Why Become a Curious Question Asker?

As a young teacher, I often heard my high school students talk about one of their favorite social studies teachers. When I asked what they liked, they told me that he taught by asking questions. That intrigued me—so different than the typical lecture-at-the-front-of-the-room approach. When I talked to my principal and mentioned that I wanted to learn more about this kind of teaching, he suggested that I observe this social studies teacher in action for a class or two.

As I sat quietly in the back of the classroom, I watched the teacher pose a question. Without hesitation, the students jumped in to discuss it from all angles. The teacher somehow managed to weave all of it together to get across the main ideas of his lesson. In this social studies class, the students certainly did not just memorize facts for the test; they lived and breathed the issues underlying that time period in history. And they loved it.

This teacher used a type of teaching called the Socratic method, named after the Greek philosopher Socrates (470–399 BC), who was known for his probing questions to get people to think. Many law schools use this method of teaching to encourage students to see both sides of an issue.[13]

I never did master this method of Socratic teaching, but I will always remember that lively classroom, brimming with engaged, curious students. And the power of a thoughtful question.

As introverts who want to live connected, we can and should tap into our natural curiosity and become skilled in asking questions.

Who do you know who asks really good questions? Could you adapt some of these questions for yourself? Have you developed a short list of questions to use in social situations as a way to help with the introvert brain freeze?

I also wonder how our friendships would bloom if we adopted Brian Grazer's practice of "Curiosity Conversations" and regularly set up a time once a month to get together with someone we admire and want to know better.

Grazer offers a few specific pointers:

- Think in advance about what you'd most hope to get out of the conversation, and think of a handful of open-ended questions that will get the person talking.
- Don't be a slave to your prepared questions. Be just the opposite: Listen closely, and be a good conversationalist. Pick up on what the person you're talking to is saying, and ask questions that expand on the stories they tell or the points they make.
- Don't share your own story or your own observations. Listen. Ask questions. The goal is for you to learn as much about the person you're talking to as you can in the time you have. If you're talking, you're not learning about the other person.[14]

And finally, what if instead of saying "Curiosity killed the cat," we lived by a new phrase: "Curiosity built the friendship"?

My friend Lara discovered that curiosity really does build a friendship.

> During the pandemic my friend Debbie posted that she was using her time during the quarantine to make T-shirt quilts for her kids. I had already decided it was a good time to start on a quilt for my eldest daughter. (For years I've rescued her T-shirts out of the giveaway bag without her knowledge.)
>
> Even with information I gathered online, I still had questions. I knew who to ask.
>
> I've known Debbie for a half-dozen years or so. At first, we connected through our children's friendship at school. But gradually our family got to know their family, and we found we enjoyed each other. A friendship between kids turned into friendships among the adults as well.

Curiosity

Now I had quilting questions for Debbie. What kind of interfacing did she use? How did she pin the layers together? Did her arms get tired while feeding the thick quilt materials through the machine? Debbie's answers revealed an ingenuity I'd never seen in her before: use duct tape to hold the backing to the floor while pinning the layers; try grippy, dollar store gloves to help feed the fabric more easily.

As a self-reliant person, I don't often ask for help, but I discovered that asking Debbie for quilting advice gave us a new and more frequent way to connect. My questions added dimension and depth to our friendship (yes, crafts can add depth). We now enjoy commiserating about the challenges involved in such a big project and celebrating our victories.[15]

As introverts who want to learn to live connected, let's keep working at letting our natural curiosity lead the way.

> **Challenge Your Introverted Self**
> Set up one of Brian Grazer's "Curiosity Conversations" with someone you have admired from afar. Rather than asking for an hour, suggest a shorter time, maybe thirty minutes, over a cup of coffee. And bring a notebook and pen with you to take notes and give yourself an eye-contact breather. Come with a few nonthreatening questions related to employment, location, family, friends, or favorite food.

And curiosity lays the groundwork for another friendship-building tool: the ability to put ourselves in someone else's shoes—empathy.

Journaling Questions

Before you dive into learning about empathy in the next chapter, take some time to answer these questions and think about the role of curiosity in your relationships.

1. How do you typically respond when someone asks the "deep" questions? How does your response affect your friendships?
2. Did you grow up in a home that feared curiosity or embraced it? What do you think now?
3. What do you think about the way Jesus asked questions?
4. What settings (dining table, road trip, long walk) do you find make you most receptive to deep questions? How might you invite someone into such a setting for a discussion?
5. What challenging social events do you face in the next few weeks? What questions might you take with you into those events to help you get to know people and feel more comfortable at the event?
6. How might curiosity help you nurture a cross-cultural friendship?
7. How might the phrase "Curiosity built the friendship" breathe new life into some of your relationships, including current friendships?

Chapter 5

Empathy

Healthy empathy feels alongside a person in pain, but not for them.

—Jamie D. Aten

Midway through an interview for a job at a medical facility, I asked, "What are you most looking for in the person you will hire for this position?"

"Empathy."

"Empathy?" I had expected to hear some variation of "an ability to multitask" or "a willingness to be a team player" or "experience with medical software."

But empathy? A job where kindness and thoughtfulness mattered most? A boss who wouldn't likely tell me, "You're too nice."

I got the job. And as the months evolved, I began to see why empathy mattered.

Patients came to my desk to sign in for their tests, often to find out if they had cancer or if their cancer had spread. As they worked to fill out the forms, I could often see a shaking hand, a furrowed brow, or even eyes filled with tears. My heart ached. How I wished I could offer each one of them a healed body. Of course, I could not. But I could open my eyes and ears to see and listen to their stories and try to put myself in their shoes, even for just a few minutes.

And I could use words to communicate empathy:

- "Wow! You have had quite a journey!"
- "I can only imagine how hard this must all be for you."
- "You have a lot on your plate right now."

I couldn't promise, "Everything will be fine!" And saying, "You'll get through this" felt so lightweight. I discovered that saying "Just take one day at a time" brought patients some relief. When I said it, I could see heads nod and often heard a sigh and some version of the response, "Yes. I can do this one day at a time."

Some patients didn't want a conversation. They wanted to get the paperwork and the test done as quickly as possible and get out of there. A curt answer to my initial greeting gave me a clue.

With these patients, I learned to sit quietly and give them space and time to fill out their forms. While they did that, I prayed for them, quietly in my heart and head, asking God to join them in this oh-so-hard journey.

Empathy. Or sympathy? A bit of both?

Often these days we use *empathy* and *sympathy* interchangeably, but they have different meanings. Author Belinda Bauman offers a helpful differentiation.

> *Sympathy* says, "I can't possibly know, but I care." . . . It does what is expected to stop your companion from hurting for the moment; it sends a card, gives a hug, tries to paint a silver lining on the situation. . . . It's polite civility.
>
> *Empathy* says, "I know and I care." . . . The way of empathy chooses to make itself vulnerable by connecting with something deep inside that knows those same feelings of pain, sadness, and fear.[1]

Empathy

Sympathy implies feeling pity for someone else, a fleeting emotion; *empathy* describes a sort of mirroring of another's feeling, digging deep to understand and enter into another's situation.

Both matter. But empathy seems to act as fertile soil to grow healthy relationships, even in the workplace.

Many introverts come by empathy naturally because we observe, listen, and think all the time. In fact, we can struggle with feeling overwhelmed with empathy (more on that later).

But what about those for whom empathy comes hard? A friend told me this story, related to the profession of architecture.

> As a young thirtysomething, Thea was already formidable, despite standing only 5'4" in wedge heels. Her focus, determination, and intelligence made her stand out in the architecture office I worked in, and she was very good at achieving what she perceived as the company's goals—projects that were on time, well-documented, and profitable. Time and time again, the unglamorous jobs she led were in the black and finished in time frames that seemed impossible. She drove her team hard, was articulate about her expectations and disappointments, and was good at managing her managers, outspoken and unafraid.
>
> Yet people kept leaving her team. Sometimes in tears, sometimes in expletive-laden rants. She was too demanding, too negative, always pushing for more, never happy with the progress that had been made. Her temper and her high expectations turned people off, but it seemed to me that it was more than that. Architecture, after all, is full of giant egos and big drama, and any leader has to make significant demands of their staff to accomplish the work required. It's a tough field for tough people.
>
> Things got bad, both for the office and for Thea. Several of us were asked to write a peer review for her, and the results must have been hard for her to hear. She understood

that she needed to change her behavior somehow, to connect in a more human way with people at work, and she tried. She said good morning, asked how someone's weekend had been. She bit her lip instead of raising her voice when she was frustrated. It was definitely better, but no one really acknowledged these efforts, maybe because they felt artificial, forced.

Then, many months later, Thea began to appear genuinely happier, less easily frustrated. People weren't leaving her teams anymore, and she started having less forced conversations, started making less forceful reprimands. As one of her peers, I noticed the change and remarked on how much better things seemed for her. It was a phone conversation, but I felt like I could hear her smiling as she told me about the change.

Many well-meaning people in the profession had given her some bad advice, she said. They had told her that to do well, she needed to be tough, and that to be heard, she would need to shout over others. What she had discovered was that the tough, outspoken energy she had didn't need to eclipse another talent she had—the ability to understand someone else's feelings and to connect with them. In fact, the two approaches were complementary and necessary. Human beings operate on trust, and we trust only when we feel connected to others. In the world of architecture, still a male- and testosterone-dominated field, it is surprising and ironic that the ability to feel and connect to others' feelings is such a powerful quality, regardless of one's gender.

Thea still gets some bad press from her previous incarnation at the office. Some people are unlikely to give the benefit of the doubt after feeling attacked. I admire her strength in taking the critical feedback that she did, but even more I admire the way she has embraced empathy as a way to connect in a real way with her teams and office. She'll be just fine.[2]

Ah, the power of empathy!

Empathy

For much of my life, I have viewed my empathic leanings as a liability. Slowly, I've begun to see empathy as a strength worth cultivating in both the workplace and in building friendships, introvert-style.

> **Introvert Inclinations**
> Appreciate a slower rhythm to life that provides time to think and pay attention to others and the world around them.
> Can tap into their vivid imaginations to help them think about other people's situations.
> Take the time to notice body language cues and listen for pain.

Imagination-Infused Empathy

Many years ago my daughter and I found ourselves at an airport, waiting out a storm. As we watched lightning streak through the sky and heard thunder rumbling throughout Dulles Airport, we fell into observing our fellow passengers. And we began to imagine their stories.

That older woman with the green jacket and graying hair had perhaps just visited her daughter and grandchildren. Now she prepared to return to her quiet life in the suburbs where she worked as a librarian. She didn't really want to return to her life, but as a recent widow, she needed the money.

We continued to exercise our vivid imaginations, between games of Uno, and thoroughly enjoyed our long wait. Our create-a-backstory game helped me think about other people and realize that they had lives and inconveniences and real struggles just as I did. My own frustration began to shrink a bit.

When we finally landed in Chicago and collected our luggage, I felt as if I knew these people. I felt sad to say goodbye to them and hoped that joy lay ahead for them.

And yet I had never spoken to any of these passengers!

A good way to develop empathy muscles? Maybe.

The histories my daughter and I had invented for these people might contain some fragments of truth, based on what we had seen and overheard, but quite possibly we had created entirely inaccurate backstories for them based primarily on our own life experiences.

As we introverts with lively imaginations seek to practice empathy, we must take care to notice when we project our life experiences and feelings onto others and make assumptions and judgments about them. That doesn't build connection. Neither does misreading another's body language.

> **Introvert Impediments**
> Can rely too much on their vivid imaginations instead of real, spoken words.
> Tend to internalize emotions rather than talking them through with someone.
> Can feel others' pain too deeply and struggle to separate others' emotions from their own.

Body Language Miscues

In 2014 *Sesame Street* produced a delightfully quirky musical parody of *Les Miserables*, titled "Les Mousserables," focused on helping kids (and their adults) to develop empathy.

Empathy

Rated ME (for mixed emotions), the parody features Jean Bon-Bon (Cookie Monster) and some rousing musical numbers, including, "Do You Hear the Cookie Crunch?" Jean Bon-Bon muddles his way through looking at other people's faces and actions and listening to their words in an attempt to act empathetically toward others. (He does eat a few cookies along the way!)

At one point Jean Bon-Bon spots a Muppet hanging her head, weeping, and hugging herself. He determines, "She bored."[3]

Oops.

Body language cues can really help in understanding another person, but they can't ever tell the whole picture.

One night after dinner as John and I talked about our days, I launched into an explanation of something I had learned about empathy. After a few minutes, John started to rub his forehead and eyes.

I looked at John and said, "Are you bored? I can stop talking."

"No."

"But you're rubbing your forehead and eyes. I just read something about body language, and I think it said when someone does that, the person is bored."

John grimaced and said, "Or it could mean someone's eyes itch."

True!

So helpful to "use our words" and not rely on assumptions, even if we think we have the ability to read body language cues well and also possess an innate ability to empathize with others.

Empathy and Genetics

During the COVID-19 pandemic, health experts urged the entire world to adopt a posture of empathy, to think about the elderly and at-risk people in our midst and what they needed to stay well, and then to act compassionately toward them by staying home.

Will we, I wonder, look back on the pandemic and agree collectively that it made us more empathetic? I hope so.

Many psychological researchers have written about mirror neurons, something in our brains that helps us recognize and copy the behavior and emotional responses of others, essentially practicing empathy. This happens with children when they see empathy in the faces of their caregivers.[4]

But what if you didn't have empathetic caregivers? Can you still learn to practice empathy? Most experts say yes, at least to some degree.

Regardless of how we come to learning and practicing empathy, we can't do it well until we first become aware and in tune with our own emotions.

Over the last few years, I've begun a practice of taking my emotional temperature throughout the day—more challenging than I realized. Do I feel overwhelmed, anxious, inadequate, frustrated, angry, excited, energized? Why? Instead of trying to shove aside those emotions, I try to greet them and understand them almost as if they appeared in a math textbook.

This process has given me more bandwidth for empathy because it alerts me when I have overstepped my abilities to carry other people's emotions. For example, when I recognize that I have entered a loop of anxiety related to a friend's health crisis, I force myself to step back from it and look at it like a math problem.

Why do I feel this way? What can I do? Do I really help anyone by staying in this loop of anxiety? I try to push pause. Finally, I gather the whole looped-anxiety mess in my hands and ask God to help me let go of it and trust Him to intervene and do what only He can do. (Like taking a strong antibiotic, I often have to do this several times a day.)

Practicing empathy sounds like a lot of effort, doesn't it? So much easier to "stay in my lane" and in my own head (an introvert's happy place).

Empathy Inconvenience

Why get involved with someone else's distress? After all, we all have our own stuff. And what can one person really do? Maybe more than we realize, as this story from my brother-in-law, Tom, reveals:

> My wife and I were driving home on an ordinary summer evening a few years ago. It was just past sundown and would soon be dark. We lived a few blocks off a busy four-lane avenue, and as we neared the turn to our street, we passed a man on the sidewalk in a manual wheelchair. It looked like he was struggling to get it moving. Ellen circled the car back around and dropped me off a little way behind him so I could signal her to continue on if it turned out the man needed help getting back to his home. When I got out of the car, I noticed a beautiful full moon over the eastern horizon. I didn't think much of it and walked up to the man to ask if he needed help. He turned to look up at me, and with the nicest smile on an obviously kind face he said, "Yeah, I do. I'm stuck." First impressions and all that: I immediately liked this person and even felt a kindred spirit. I said, "Okay, I'll try to help. By the way, my name is Tom." He beamed and said, "My name's Tom too!" We shook hands, and I asked what to do. He asked me to try pulling the wheel out of the crack it was in. Done.

Living Connected

Tom lived in an apartment building about ten blocks away and said "Sure" when I asked if he wanted me to push him home because it was getting dark. I signaled thumbs-up to my wife, and we started on our way. After a minute I asked, "Hey Tom, can I turn you around for a second? There's a beautiful full moon behind us." We turned and paused a moment to take it in and then continued along the sidewalk. Conversation was easy. We discovered we liked a lot of the same music.

At his apartment, I peeked inside and noticed some art on the walls and a huge collection of CDs by his sound system. I said, "Hey, maybe I could come by sometime, and we could listen to music together." We exchanged phone numbers.

Over the past five years, Tom has become one of my closest friends. We get together almost every week and talk about everything. We've been to rock concerts, restaurants, and Lake Michigan, but mostly we just order food and hang out at each other's houses for a couple hours. Sometimes, when we see a full moon, we reminisce about that night and comment on how lucky we were to have crossed paths like we did.[5]

We can so easily squelch our empathetic impulses, telling ourselves, *I'm too busy.* Or *I'm just not equipped to navigate this situation.* Or *I'm not good at hard stuff. Shouldn't friendship feel easy?*

The Old Testament Book of Nehemiah tells another remarkable story of empathy. The prophet Nehemiah and many other Jews had been captured by the Babylonians and forced to leave their beloved Jerusalem and live far away.

Yet Nehemiah never forgot his homeland. When he heard that things had been going downhill in Jerusalem, including the destruction of the wall that protected the city, he responded with empathy: "When I heard this, I sat down and wept. In fact, for days I mourned, fasted, and prayed to the God of heaven" (Nehemiah 1:4).

I find Nehemiah's response to this revelation fascinating, given that he lived far away in a posh palace, working as King Artaxerxes's trusted cupbearer. He had a good life.

And yet he also had empathy.

When Nehemiah explained his troubled heart to King Artaxerxes, the king offered resources for Nehemiah to return to Jerusalem and help his countrymen rebuild the wall, which they did in a record fifty-two days.

Nehemiah could easily have sent someone in his stead. He could have said, "I'm so busy and important, I just can't take on anything else." He could have shut his eyes and ears and just gone about his daily responsibilities. He could have said, "I'll pray and fast. That is enough." Instead, he let his empathy urge him toward acting with compassion.

Interesting to notice that this massive construction project launched with many days of prayer and fasting.

As Nehemiah opened his heart to God in honest prayer, it seems that God began to shape Nehemiah's heart to reflect God's own heart for Jerusalem. And those times of prayer also developed within Nehemiah a heart of compassion, not judgment, for the people in Jerusalem.

Prayer and empathy make such a powerful combination.

An Empathetic Friendship Prompt

In *Storm Sisters* I wrote about a group of women with whom I went to college and who remain my dear friends. We live scattered around the world, but we stay in touch through emails, phone calls, texts, and long weekends now and then. Lately, we have discovered that texting works well. Just last night I received two texts: "Please pray . . ." I've sent out many of those texts myself.

What I so love about these texts, and this commitment to pray for one another, is that we get to watch God show up. I can't tell you how many times I've checked my texts to read, "God answered our prayers" (accompanied, of course, with lots of emojis and exclamation points).

Thankfully, prayer can happen anytime and anywhere, even through text messages. It need not happen only in the quiet of a church service or around a dinner table or in the before-sunrise hush of a new day.

Consider these suggestions:

- On the way to work each morning (or before you start your workday from home), pray for each of your coworkers by name, maybe even out loud.
- Designate one day a week to pray for your social media contacts or develop a daily social-media habit of reading and then praying, perhaps even writing out a prayer in the comments.
- As you walk in your neighborhood, pray for your neighbors.
- As you drive by the homes of friends or the businesses where friends work, pray for them.
- As you answer emails, for work or for pleasure, pray for the recipient after you push send.

Empathy

Prayer suits my introverted soul so well. I can do it in my own quiet space in my own quiet way. No one else even needs to know about it. I can give this gift anonymously.

But a funny thing happens to me in the process of prayer—a connection thing.

As I pray for people, God gently nudges me toward them. He reminds me that I don't really know what challenges my coworkers face at home or how my neighbor fared after the recent hailstorm. He nudges me to have an in-person conversation with an email connection. Through prayer, God gives me His eyes to see the people around me and His ears to hear their stories.

Prayer prompts me to *ask* questions of the people around me and then *listen* carefully so I can pray well for them.

- What challenges loom on your horizon?
- What keeps you awake at night?

Not everyone wants to answer these questions and may choose instead to talk about the weather or daily details. But sometimes these prayer-prompted, not gossip-prompted, questions lead to an honest conversation and a developing friendship.

Over a decade ago, I watched from across the street as my neighbor, Bev, nursed her husband through a grueling fight with brain cancer. Every time I passed her house and turned into my driveway, I prayed for her family: "Lord, give them strength and your comfort. Help them in this hard, hard time." I wept at Gary's memorial service and put the order of service on my desk as a reminder to pray for Bev and her kids.

I kept praying as I walked my dog past Bev's house every morning and observed her closed door.

And then, one day, Bev got a dog, Chase, and they came out their back door to join Ringo and me on our walk around the block. She came the next day too. And the next.

My heart, primed by prayer, eagerly welcomed the company and the conversation.

Thousands of days later, we still walk together in the morning, even though my sweet Ringo has left this world. We do talk weather and daily details as well as politics and baseball, but we also talk about what keeps us up at night and the challenges we face.

Prayer for others definitely nudges us in an empathetic direction, even for those who say, "Empathy just isn't in my gene pool."

Empathy Overload

During the pandemic crisis, I found myself fighting empathy overload. My heart ached for the recent widow and surgery patient left alone to navigate life and recovery. And the friends losing loved ones and unable to gather together to celebrate their lives. And the masked people in the grocery store with eyes full of stress. And . . .

Some days all of it crashed in on my heart, particularly on rainy, gray days. I literally felt paralyzed. What could I say? What could I do? Nothing felt enough.

I can only imagine the empathy overload frontline responders must have felt.

Author Judith Orloff describes a type of person, an empath, for whom empathy runs deep, someone who can't help actually feeling what others feel. She offers some wise advice to empaths, which I also take to heart as an introvert with an active, empathetic imagination:

- Ask yourself, "Is this symptom or emotion mine or someone else's?"
  . . . Feelings are catchy, especially if they relate to a hot button issue for you. . . . The more you heal issues that trigger you, the less likely you'll be to absorb emotions from others.
- Set limits and boundaries.
  . . . "No" is a complete sentence! It's okay to tell someone, "I'm sorry, I'm not up for going to a party tonight."[6]

We can learn to practice empathy well, even we introverts who tend to live in our heads and have lively imaginations.

Empathy as a Two-Way Street

Clearly empathy can help us make connections. But the empathetic connections shouldn't always go one direction. For true friendships to develop, we need to allow others to enter into our emotions.

After talking with people about my first book, *Storm Sisters*, I realized that so many of us take great comfort in *doing* but we struggle with *receiving*. We resist letting others know our challenges and giving them the opportunity to help us or speak into our situation with words of kindness and empathy.

Adam McHugh says it so well in his book *Introverts in the Church*:

> One particularly insidious behavior in introverts is our tendency to suffer alone. We internalize our dark emotions, often increasing our loneliness and closing ourselves to the love and empathy being offered to us. For my introverted friend Emily, the most profound thing she has learned to say to others is "I'm not okay." Others are able to offer the gentleness of Christ to us when we are not able to be gentle with ourselves. God surrounded me with a chorus of gentle, introverted voices as I sought to embrace my own introversion—a spiritual director who saw God's handiwork, a therapist who helped me unravel the threads of my personality, a pastor who empathized with my ministry exhaustion, and a supervisor who gave me permission to be an introvert in an extroverted profession. They met my harsh inner critic with compassion and kindness.[7]

Should we work to practice empathetic techniques, such as listening, asking clarifying questions, watching body language, prayer? Absolutely! But we also should allow others to practice those techniques on us. And that requires us to pay attention to our own hearts.

One afternoon during the COVID-19 crisis, I called a friend I've known since college. She asked, "How are you?" I took a deep breath and gave her an honest answer. That day I felt frustrated about trying to live well with people. I explained to her that I had gotten irritated with someone I love over the weekend because we have very different approaches to dealing with stress. As I explained the different approaches, my friend said, "How does that make you feel? I think I would feel frustrated." As we continued to talk, I admitted that I did indeed feel frustrated.[12]

Linda's empathy—putting herself in my place and working to understand my thoughts and emotions—put voice to my frustration and in turn helped me find

Empathy

the words I needed to talk to this person. I found courage to own my own frustration and also talk through a compromise instead of shoving my frustration down deep into my soul and letting it fester.

Of course, Linda could never know precisely how I felt, but she could (and did) ask questions to clarify, and she could (and did) imagine herself in my situation for a few minutes. She didn't try to fix my problem by offering a quick solution, and she didn't just dismiss it and start talking about her own life. She listened with her head and her heart. And it helped!

So . . . as we work to build friendships in a quiet, thoughtful sort of way, let's remember that empathy does its best work on a two-way street.

I believe in empathy. I know that it builds relationships. I also know that it can easily overwhelm if we don't exercise it wisely and accompany it with actual, spoken words and questions and large doses of prayer.

> **Challenge Your Introverted Self**
> What challenging situation lies on your heart? Find a way to mention this to a friend-in-the-making. (Extra points if you use spoken words rather than written words!) Take note of the other person's response, but also pay attention to your response to his or her response.

Some introverts refer to empathy as their "secret sauce" for building connections. Cultivating loyalty helps too. We'll tackle that in the next chapter. But first, spend some time mulling over your thoughts about empathy with the help of these journaling questions.

Journaling Questions

1. Think about the jobs you've had. How did empathy matter or not matter?
2. What struggles do you have with practicing empathy?
3. What strategies have you developed for coping with empathy overload? Try taking your emotional temperature for a week, several times each day. Record each day in a journal. What do you notice at the end of the week?
4. Describe a time when your imagination helped or hurt you in a relationship.
5. What struggles do you have with receiving empathy?
6. What do you take away from Nehemiah's response to the plight of his people in Jerusalem?
7. How do you approach prayer? How might you begin to pray for people whom you would like to befriend? Make a prayer list of 2 or 3 people. Develop a reminder to pray—set an alarm on your phone, use visual landmarks on a walk in your neighborhood or drive to work, post something on a mirror . . .

Chapter 6

Loyalty

What sort of loyalty is there in the age of Facebook, when friendship is a costless transaction, a business of flip reciprocity (I'll go on your list of friends if you'll go on my list)?

—Eric Felten

Roberta has a knack for hanging on to people. She reminds me that *loyalty*—"the quality or state of being true and constant in support of someone or something"[1]—still can describe what happens between people not just how we feel about shoes or pizza or...

During our senior year of high school, Roberta and I met and befriended Saki, a Japanese exchange student. (Although her given name was Hisako, everyone knew her as Saki.) We cheered together at the state basketball tournament that year and enjoyed other outings. Saki sang a beautiful rendition of "You Light Up My Life," at our school talent show. At the end of the year, Roberta assembled a patchwork pillow to which we each contributed a section.

I lost track of Saki after graduation as I became wrapped up in my own college and career journey; Roberta did not. I'll let her tell the story.

> Over the next seven years, Saki and I continued a pen-pal correspondence, exchanging photos and Christmas cards. It was such a thrill to receive postmarked airmail letters from Japan!

Living Connected

In 1986, my new husband and I had the opportunity to take a group tour of Japan, and the highlight of our extended stay was spending three days with Saki and her parents at their family home. We slept on tatami mats, tried on traditional kimonos, ate sushi, and experienced life as a family member rather than as a tourist.

The warm welcome we received from Saki was life-changing and prompted Bill and me to serve as weekend homestay host parents for twenty-two Japanese college students from Mukogawa Women's University through an exchange program in our city of Spokane, Washington, over a number of years.

Our four children learned to count in Japanese, to use chopsticks, to enjoy traditional foods prepared by our students, and to experience the passion of our students' learning about American culture as well as sharing their Japanese culture.

Saki met and married a wonderful Dutch fellow, and they became the proud parents of two children, Christina and Thomas.

Raising our kids on different continents, we continued to maintain our written correspondence, which included a family photo exchange at holidays.

In 2005, Saki and her family traveled to the US, and they were able to spend a week with our family in Spokane. Their daughter, Christina, was of similar age to our youngest daughter, Lizzie, and spoke good English. Their six-year-old son, Thomas, spoke limited English, but he and our son Michael, age nine, both competed at XBox video games. "I win, you lose" was one of Thomas's few English phrases.

We endeavored to reciprocate the hospitality that Saki and her parents had shown to Bill and me in Japan by planning simple activities such as a trip to Silverwood (Old West-style) Theme Park, making tie-dyed T-shirts, painting a ceramic platter, and barbecuing and camping in the backyard.

Our daughter, Lizzie, and Saki's daughter, Christina, became pen pals, and later, Facebook friends.

Loyalty

As our forty-year high school reunion drew close, I eagerly hoped Saki could attend. But then, much to my surprise, I received word through Christina that the world lost a bright light when Saki passed away suddenly in 2019. My heart deeply misses her.

In 2020 I learned that Saki's daughter would be a research fellow at Stanford University. Bill and I had organized a family reunion in San Diego, California, for that year so we asked Christina if she would like to meet our family for three days.

We had fun going to the San Diego Zoo, exploring tide pools and the beach, playing card games, playing ball with our two-year-old granddaughter, and learning about Christina's research project on Alzheimer's and brain aging at Stanford. She is an accomplished and articulate young woman, so much like her mother. It was so nice to reconnect after fifteen years!

Who knew that a friendship begun in high school would turn into a connection that spanned generations, international boundaries, and decades?[2]

Loyalty mattered to Roberta in high school and it still does, despite her responsibilities of a family and a career.

When life gets full, I can easily get overwhelmed with day-to-day survival, and as an introvert, I seem to have a people quota. Relationship-building requires such effort and nuance for everyone, but for introverts, who happily spend time alone, it can so easily feel utterly exhausting.

I want to let loyalty infuse my relationships and grow them over days and years and decades. But how?

Introverts Have a Loyalty Quota

When I think of acting as a loyal friend, I want it to mean remembering my friend's important dates, communicating faithfully, speaking words of encouragement and challenge, praying specifically, showing up routinely, and even responding to the 2 a.m. phone call for help. Whew! Overwhelming and time-consuming! And maybe just a tad bit unrealistic.

Just how many people can an introvert fit into his or her life? Seriously.

Author Eric Felten reminds me that we do all have a loyalty quota. He writes, "Real friendship entails not just contact but a range of obligations, an implicit guarantee that we will come through for our pals whenever their moment of crisis may come. It also means favoring the interests of your friends—taking a stake in their interests. *How many people's divergent desires can we embrace before we're no longer embracing anyone's particular interests?*"[3]

Have you thought about your loyalty quota? How many people can you "go deep" with? Really. As an introvert.

Take a moment now and make a list of all the people you call "friend." Include your spouse and family members.

Now put a star in front of the names of people who matter most to you. Let these questions help you figure that out.

- With whom do I communicate frequently?
- Who is having the greatest influence on my thinking?
- Whom do I want to be like?[4]

Perhaps you find yourself in a season of life where you don't have many people in your life. Try making a list of the people you once had in your life. Put a star by the names of people who used to matter most to you.

How many people did you star? Half a dozen? A dozen? One?

Does that number feel too much? Too little? Just right? Just what is your loyalty quota?

As we work through the rest of the chapter, keep in mind the person or people you starred and ask yourself, *How might I employ loyalty as a way to nurture this relationship?*

And remember, loyalty will not always look the same way in every friendship or potential friendship.

Author Shasta Nelson says it well: "We understand on some important level that not every relationship needs to be that close in order to still be healthy, significant, meaningful, or helpful. This isn't an all-or-nothing game. It's not best friend or bust."[5]

Of course, our loyalty quota may change depending on the season of life we find ourselves in. Doing a periodic loyalty-quota audit makes sense.

And so does recognizing that loyalty starts in our heads.

Loyalty Begins in Thought

A writer-friend of mine once published a short piece that set me on edge. I actually agreed with the content but not so much the delivery. I fired off a rather strident email explaining how the piece had hurt me and muttered to myself, "Why should I keep supporting this author?"

We emailed a bit and had a clarifying phone call. I began to realize that I had misunderstood some of the piece and that it had hit a nerve—pointing out something I needed to address. I also discovered why this topic mattered so much to my writer-friend.

Why so much effort? I could just have stopped reading and supporting this author on social media and let my angry, hurt emotions win.

Why try to talk this through?

Loyalty.

I've read a lot of words from this writer-friend, including some that have changed me significantly. I can't forget that in a moment of frustration. If I remind myself to "assume the best and talk about the rest," I focus on the fact that this author has a track record of wise, faith-filled words and a writing style infused with passion. I also remind myself that living in a world ripe with riots and a pandemic puts all of us on edge.

I may not always agree with this writer's point of view, but I certainly can let loyalty lead the way in laying the foundation for a supportive relationship.[6]

The Bible contains some well-known stories of loyalty between friends: Jonathan and David; Ruth and Naomi; Paul and Barnabas. It also contains a story that oozes with loyalty in a messy sort of way. In the Book of Job, we read about a man who struggles with loyalty in his connection to God and also in his connection to friends. Reading it makes me uncomfortable.

As I recently read the entire Book of Job, I found myself muttering under my breath at Job's friends, "Really? How could you say that?" (Similar to what I said to my writer-friend.)

At the beginning of the story of Job, his friends came and just sat with him, saying nothing. But then something flipped the on-switch to their tongues, and they heaped their words of "wisdom" on Job.

One friend, Eliphaz, confidently explained:

Loyalty

> There's no limit to your sins.
> "For example, you must have lent money to your friend
>   and demanded clothing as security.
>   Yes, you stripped him to the bone.
> You must have refused water for the thirsty
>   and food for the hungry.
> You probably think the land belongs to the powerful
>   and only the privileged have a right to it!
> You must have sent widows away empty-handed
>   and crushed the hopes of orphans.
> That is why you are surrounded by traps
>   and tremble from sudden fears.
> That is why you cannot see in the darkness,
>   and waves of water cover you.
>   Job 22:5-11 (emphasis mine)

What a pile of assumptions and, ironically, uttered with the intent to help Job feel better!

I cringe when I read these words because I see myself in them. I can so easily make assumptions about what other people have done or not done and then believe that they have created their own current difficult situation.

What if Job's friends had adopted the loyalty principle of "believe the best and talk about the rest" instead of making unfounded assumptions?

What if we determined to do the same?

We introverts, who live so easily in our heads, can forget to make the effort to "use our words" to ask a clarifying question instead of making a sweeping accusation.

We can assume that getting no response to a text means we have somehow angered a friend when in reality it might mean that our friend lost his phone.

We can assume that a friend who forgets our birthday just no longer cares when in reality that friend might find herself up to her ears in family or personal issues.

We can assume that silence on the subject of racial injustice means lack of interest when in fact it might mean a desire to develop a broader understanding before speaking.

When we have a track record with someone—years of observed responses to situations—we have good reason to "assume the best," but when we have just begun to connect with someone, "assuming the best" comes harder. But it matters just as much. If we allow ourselves to drift into assuming the worst of everyone we meet, why would we ever risk connection? And if we allow those negative thoughts to spill out in conversations with others, we erect so many hurdles in the long-distance race of friendship.

So, think back to your list of people with whom you would like to practice loyalty. How have your thoughts or assumptions helped or hindered the growth of this relationship? What might you do differently?

> **Introvert Inclinations**
> Find social media an enjoyable place to connect with others because it does not involve face-to-face contact and often revolves around words.
> Understand the value of thoughts and words.
> Value deep connections, especially long-term relationships steeped in loyalty.

Loyalty Shows in Words

Have you ever had a friend who routinely tells you what irritates her about her other friends? As she tells you about the crazy or hurtful thing her friend did, do you find yourself wondering, *What does she tell her friends about* me?

Maybe, just maybe, you've done this yourself. I have. Sigh! More often than I'd like to admit. My introverted personality leads me to think and analyze constantly. Without much effort, I can drift into critical analysis of situations with friends and then share my insights with others.

Not exactly loyalty.

So how do we learn to use our words to build friendships, steeped in loyalty, especially when we continually rub shoulders with imperfect people (including ourselves)?

Over our thirty-plus years of marriage, John and I have talked a lot about the people in our lives and how to live well with them. He tends easily toward the glass-half-full view of life and people. I can easily drift into the glass-half-empty mentality. But even with John's positive attitude, he still encounters people-frustration. As we talk through people situations, one of us often says quietly, "Matthew 18."

That has become code for, *You need to go talk directly to this person.*

Matthew 18:15 (NIV) states, "If your brother or sister sins, go and point out their fault, just between the two of you. If they listen to you, you have won them over."

Loyalty: *rather than talking to someone else about something another person did to hurt me, I will talk directly to that person.* Such a conversation can lead to change and a deeper connection, or it can lead to distance with a person who just doesn't want to discuss hard things or see the need for change.

> **Introvert Impediments**
> Can get stuck in our own internal conversations.
> Can drift into critical analysis of others.
> Creatively find ways to avoid uncomfortable situations.

I wonder how adopting this principle in the workplace would play out.

Stephen Covey, author of the best-selling *7 Habits of Highly Effective People*, says, "Being loyal to those who are absent and assuming good faith of others are keys to building trust in a culture. . . . When you defend the integrity of a person who is absent, what does that say to those who are present? It says that you would do the same thing for them."[7]

What a great reminder (and challenge) to commit to saying only words about someone that you wouldn't mind them overhearing.

And now, the elephant in the room—social media. How do we practice loyalty on social media?

During the pandemic, I saw and heard so many stories of friendships, church members, and even families splintering over impassioned Facebook exchanges about political issues, racial issues, and even medical concerns, such as the wearing of masks. So many of us felt compelled to share our opinions.

Loyalty

Does that build relationships? Maybe, if both parties listen respectfully. But does our use of social media really foster an environment of listening?

What if we took a loyalty-based approach to social media?

- Have one-on-one conversations via Zoom or phone about politics, race, medicine, religion, etc.?
- Listen and pray as we scroll through social media?
- Take regular fasts from social media and use that time to connect individually with people?

What if loyalty overtook our social media accounts in the form of: "Assume the best and talk about the rest (in private)?"

Especially for we introverts, social media can truly help build friendships. We don't have to engage in small talk in a crowded room; we can pop in and out as we feel equipped; we can connect with a wide range of people from all areas of our lives.

During the pandemic I got mad at social media. I just couldn't handle the barrage of words, many of them angry and negative. I deleted all the apps on my phone and slipped into social media silence. Ah!

A few weeks after my social media shut-down, I began to hear about things through email or text that I had missed—birthdays, events, book launches . . . I realized that for me, practicing loyalty on social media means I need to stay on it. Sigh! But I need to manage it better so it doesn't manage me. I still don't have the apps on my phone, and I have set boundaries on the time I spend on social media.

Seems that loyalty for me means not giving up entirely on social media but instead committing to use it well to connect. I'll keep at it. And take periodic breaks to recalibrate.

Thinking back to those people or person you listed with whom you want to practice loyalty, how could you strengthen this relationship by using words differently, particularly on social media?

Loyalty Requires Action

We introverts thrive in the worlds of thoughts and words but can struggle with putting feet to our good-intentioned thoughts and words.

I may work hard to *think* the best of a friend or a friend-to-be and try to *speak* well of her to others and on social media, but how do I *show* her that I want to build a friendship or deepen the friendship we already have?

Time to *do* something—to let my loyalty show.

Does that mean telling every friend or potential friend that I'll show up to help them at 2 a.m.?

I don't think so. Truthfully, I could never sustain that kind of commitment, especially as an introvert. But I can do other things, simple things, loyal things, that show my desire for connection.

Regular communication, even once a year, certainly displays loyalty and can grow a friendship in small increments.

So can showing up in someone else's life in quiet, thoughtful sorts of way.

- Say something about important events, such as the anniversary of a loss, personal milestones, transitions...
- Pray. After talking to friends, take time pray for them or with them.

Loyalty

- Commit to a small group of some kind (online or in person) and show up every time on time with a heart to "assume the best . . ." about other group members.

Some friends of mine struggled with a small group commitment. They told me this story:

> There was a person in the group who was not like the others. This person dominated conversations, was opinionated (sometimes cruelly so), and not respectful of other people's time. Truthfully, we didn't "like" this person in our group. And it became an ongoing concern.
> We considered quitting, taking our ball and going home.
> But we couldn't forget that God had chosen to draw these people together in a small group and in Christ. And we couldn't forget that God loved *us* despite who *we* are.
> We knew we must ask God to help us choose to love even when we couldn't "like."
> God has not "kicked us to the curb" despite our many flaws, so we determined to do our best to imitate Him.
> Things didn't instantly become "happily ever after" in our small group once we made that choice. But we didn't do it with the hope of gaining something wonderful. We did it in response to God's loyalty to us.[8]

I watched and listened as my friends wrestled through this struggle with their small group. And I noticed that as they practiced loyalty, sticking with people, their hearts and faith grew larger and deeper. I marveled. And admitted that I probably would have walked away.

Confession here: I avoid small groups. As an introvert, I find them overwhelming. When do I talk? How do I connect with people honestly? What if we just don't get along?

After talking with these friends and several others about the life-giving connections they have found in small groups by staying loyal to the people in the group despite personal differences, I know I need to look for a small group opportunity. I need to work on practicing loyalty in deed. Even as an introvert.

Thinking back to those people or person you listed with whom you want to practice loyalty, what one deed could you do this month to demonstrate your loyalty (and interest) in this relationship?

Loyalty Can Hurt

Learning to stick it out with challenging group members can often bring growth to all members as they learn to live out loyalty. But what about practicing loyalty in a relationship where the other person practices self-destructive behaviors, such as refusing to address mental health issues, regularly exploding in tirades of physical or emotional abuse, or turning to substances to deal with struggles?

I've had so many conversations with men and women who lived for twenty or more years in a physically and emotionally abusive marriage because they wanted to stay loyal to this person they married.

Certainly, loyalty should never trump safety in any relationship. And certainly, loyalty in any relationship should lay the groundwork for a "please-get-help" conversation. Dr. John Townsend says it this way: "To tell a good friend, 'I want you to see a therapist to get some help on this' is one of the most growth-producing things anyone can do."[9]

"Assume the best and talk about the rest" sounds good, but it can definitely backfire in a relationship

Loyalty

with one or more unhealthy people who don't willingly want to talk things through and adjust.

My friend Connie has a big, loyal heart. She recently told me this story:

> My friend Sharon and I had been close friends locally for about fifteen years, having kids of similar age and families that enjoyed being together. When Sharon's family decided to attend a church closer to their home, I believed our friendship would continue, though it also was clear and right that they would make new friendships too. Over the next couple years, we kept in touch, though we talked and saw each other less and less.
>
> Then Sharon's doctor found a malignant tumor, and I wanted to stand by her side. I offered several times to go to treatments with her and bring a meal by for her family. While she thanked me for the offers, she did not need either the company or the food.
>
> A little disappointed, I recognized that she was going through a hard thing, and she had the right to decide what was really of help to her. Her treatments progressed and she recovered.
>
> Over time, it became clear that Sharon was not interested in continuing our friendship.
>
> I don't think I made any demands on her or neglected to care for her. I can't explain it but do feel sad about it.[10]

How I wish Connie and Sharon had found a way to talk about expectations and changes and challenges. But I admire Connie for admitting her regret and also graciously letting go of this friendship and not wallowing in the pain of rejection or feeling paralyzed to extend loyalty to other people in a gesture of friendship.

In order for loyalty to do its best work and grow a friendship, it has to matter to both people. One friend who continually practices undying loyalty cannot carry an entire relationship. Healthy relationships, whether in marriage or friendship, require two healthy, committed people.

God's Loyalty Motivates

In my reading of the Book of Job, I couldn't help but notice Job's verbal wrestling match with God. At first, in the midst of layer upon layer of loss and grief, Job refused to curse God, even when his wife said to him, "'Are you still trying to maintain your integrity? Curse God and die.' But Job replied, 'You talk like a foolish woman. Should we accept only good things from the hand of God and never anything bad?' So in all, this Job said nothing wrong" (Job 2:9-10).

As the story continues and the suffering mounts, Job's words take on a different tone. Chapter 21 records his anger at God: "My complaint is with God, not with people" (verse 4) and "Who is the Almighty, and why should we obey him? What good will it do us to pray?" (verse 15).

Then we read God's response in chapters 40-41. He calls out Job's lack of understanding about the world and suffering and God's character and abilities. Ouch!

Job responds,

> I know that you can do anything,
>   and no one can stop you.
> You asked, 'Who is this that questions my wisdom with such ignorance?'
>   It is I—and I was talking about things I knew nothing about,
>   things far too wonderful for me.
>
> I take back everything I said,
>   and I sit in dust and ashes to show my repentance.
>
> Job 42:1-3, 6

Loyalty

God and Job, after several rounds of verbal sparring, restored their relationship.

I love that God did not abandon Job utterly, disgusted with Job's verbal thrashing and anguished doubt.

And I love that Job did not abandon God, despite God calling him out for his ignorance.

Loyalty.

Job and God did not give up on each other. They talked through really hard stuff and salvaged their relationship. That motivates me. I want to remember this messy story of Job as I navigate my own messy relationships and seek to "assume the best and talk about the rest."

How I love hearing that loyalty does still exist in our world—loyalty to people not just to brands. Amy reminded me of this by telling me about her not-always-easy friendship with a woman she met in college.

> I met Dawn as a freshman our first week on campus. We lived on the same floor and quickly discovered that we had chosen similar majors. As we spent time together, I felt drawn to her enthusiasm for life, sense of humor, and love for God.
>
> We decided to room together sophomore year and every year after that.
>
> I couldn't afford to fly home to the East Coast over Thanksgiving, so Dawn invited me to spend the holiday with her family who lived locally. Dawn's mom quickly became my second mom.
>
> After graduation, Dawn sang "Ave Maria" at our wedding and served as one of my bridesmaids. I still remember the sound of her beautiful soprano voice filling the church. She had a gift.
>
> Dawn met a man during college. When I questioned her multiple times about the hasty relationship, she listened but insisted on marrying this man anyway. I agreed to be a bridesmaid. And when she had a son, I also joyfully agreed to be his godmother.

Then Dawn hit some hard years, including a divorce, a myriad of health issues, a move home to live with her parents, and a second hasty marriage. We stayed in touch through frequent, sometimes challenging, phone calls.

When Dawn told me one day that she had been diagnosed with kidney disease and needed a transplant, I wanted to help. I jumped on a plane to Mayo Clinic to get tested for a possible kidney donation. Sadly, my kidney did not prove to be a match for Dawn.

Eventually, Dawn's kidneys failed completely. After three unsuccessful transplants, the Lord called her home to Heaven on October 1996. I read Scripture and spoke at her funeral. And I committed myself to stay in touch with her son, whom I think of as my third son.

To honor Dawn's love of music, her parents and I established an endowed scholarship fund to benefit future music education majors at our alma mater.[11]

Dawn and Amy developed a 2-a.m.-phone-call-for-help sort of relationship—a gift for them both, birthed in loyalty despite some challenging life events.

Even we introverts need one friend like this.

One day, while working on this chapter, I reached for a favorite book on my bookshelf: *Bridge to Terabithia* by Katherine Paterson—a tender story of loyalty between two children. I thought I had bought this copy for a class in college on children's literature, but when I opened the book, I discovered an inscription: "Afton, May God bless you in your writing and reading that you do for Him! I love you! Jody."

The date on that inscription was 1981!

When I texted Jody photos of the book and the inscription, she replied quickly, "Still do pray for you!!"[12]

Oh, my! The tears came—happy tears, grateful tears. What a gift of loyalty—decades of faithful prayer that call out the gifts of a friend.

Loyalty

And that's what loyalty can do, even between two introverts who first met in a college dorm as teenagers.

Feel up to practicing loyalty one small thought, word, or deed at a time and laying the groundwork for a lifelong friendship? I hope so.

> **Challenge Your Introverted Self**
> Find a small group to join for just six weeks. Commit to showing up (online or in person) for every session. Keep a journal about your journey. What stretches you? How does it feel to practice loyalty by showing up? How did your connections with other group members develop or not develop? How did the experience change you? Would you do it again?

We'll talk about another word in the next chapter that puts some practical legs to this concept of loyalty: *confidentiality*.

But before we move on to another word, press pause and think (or journal) about these questions.

Journaling Questions

1. How has loyalty served you in building relationships?
2. How has acting "too loyally" affected your relationships negatively?
3. What does loyalty mean to you as an introvert?
4. When you hit a snag with another person, how often do you talk to someone else about it rather than talking to the person who offended you? Why?

5. Think of a situation where things went askew in a friendship. How might applying the Matthew 18 principle have brought healing to this friendship?
6. How do you respond to knowing that God did not give up on Job?

Chapter 7

Confidentiality

These matters are always a secret, till it is found out that every body knows them.

—Mr. Weston (*Emma* by Jane Austen)

I still cringe when I remember a Christmas letter I sent out many years ago.

That year I had watched a dear friend wrestle through some health issues that led to the diagnosis of a rare disease. I didn't know what to say or how to help. And I felt so sad. So what did I do? I mentioned my friend's struggle in my Christmas letter. Really!

What was I thinking?!

I wish I knew!

Looking back now, I realize that I had no business telling my friend's story. This story belonged to her, not to me. She, and only she, should have determined how and when the story unfolded for other people.

Imagine her shock when she pulled out my letter.

My friend easily could have decided she simply couldn't trust me, and our friendship could have imploded. Thankfully, she continued to believe the best about me.

I wish I could say I never did anything like this ever again. But I did. Sigh!

When my mom received her diagnosis of Creutzfeldt-Jakob disease, a rare, hideous, always-fatal brain disease, I flailed. What would the days ahead hold? How could we help Mom?

I sent out a "help!" email.

Good instinct to reach for people? Yes. But in doing so I also shared my mom's story, something she had hoped to keep quiet as long as possible.

My email upset Mom, understandably. If only I had found a way to reach for help and also protect my mom's privacy.

Clearly, confidentiality ("the state of keeping or being kept secret or private"[1]) matters in relationships and can often make or break them.

Practically speaking, confidentiality means saying to someone, *I'm a vault; what you tell me stays with me. I won't share it without your permission.*

Much to my chagrin, I've learned that holding the confidences of another takes concerted thought and effort. What a challenge to know something about another person and deliberately choose not to pass on that tidbit, to remember, *Not my story!*

Before we jump in to talk about this delicate topic, we need to push pause for a minute and agree that safety comes first. If someone confides in you about abuse or suicidal thoughts, you must NOT stay silent. And if you find yourself in such a dangerous situation, please do confide in a trusted friend and please do not disown that friend when he or she breaks your confidence in order to save your life. Safety trumps confidentiality.

A Culture of Confidentiality?

Interestingly, we care so much about *confidentiality* here in America that in 1996 we passed a federal law: The Health Insurance Portability and Accountabili-

Confidentiality

ty Act (HIPAA). It established "national standards to protect sensitive patient health information from being disclosed without the patient's consent or knowledge."[2] We can't see a doctor or have surgery without having a signed HIPAA document on file.

Because I worked in healthcare, I agreed to abide by HIPAA and carefully protect patient information. I continually got warnings on my work computer that I should NOT look at a patient's chart unless I had a medical reason to do so. I could lose my job if I started poking around in a friend's or neighbor's medical chart.

HIPAA also came into play on days when I worked at a check-in desk and saw a patient I knew. After a friendly greeting, I said, "Just so you know, because of HIPAA, I won't say anything to anyone I know about your visit here."

Imagine if I went out to dinner with friends and happened to mention the name of a person I had just seen in my waiting room for a brain MRI. What if my friend replied, "That is my boss!" I have now created a situation for both my friend and my friend's boss. And I can never erase those words once they've come out of my mouth.

That imaginary situation perfectly portrays the idiom, *breach of confidentiality*: "failure to respect a person's privacy by telling another person private information."[3] Eek!

Not my story to tell.

My friend, Jennifer Stenzel works as a licensed clinical professional counselor and deals with confidentiality issues every time she meets with a client.

Because I work with teens, they often ask, "Won't you just run and tell my mom and dad?"

I say, "If I did not guarantee you confidentiality, you would not take the risk to talk to me."

They still ask, "Are you sure you're not going to tell my parents?"

I respond, "I really care about you, but I don't want to lose my license."

As a counselor I have a standard of ethics I have to maintain. If I breach these ethics, including confidentiality, someone can make a complaint about me before an ethics board. And I could lose my license.

Of course, we must say something in situations of physical and emotional harm, such as suicide or homicide—a safety risk. The safety rule is applicable in friendship as well.

This is what confidentiality looks like out in the real world: I tell all my clients, "I'll look at you as if I don't know you if I see you at Starbucks or anywhere else. If you smile at me, I'll smile back."

Otherwise, if I saw a teenaged client at a Starbucks talking to a friend, and I said hi, that friend of my client might say, "Who is that woman?" That creates an awkward moment for my client.

It can be sort of funny sometimes. I'll be at something, maybe a cocktail party, and someone will introduce me to someone who is my client. I'll say hello and act as if this person is a stranger to me.[4]

I wonder what would happen to our American culture if we instituted a federal privacy law that prohibited us from telling secrets about other people—telling their stories without their permission. Perhaps an NMS law—Not My Story.

A Culture of Gossip?

If *confidentiality* means keeping personal information private, then the word *gossip* defines the opposite approach, talking to another person (or people) about someone not in the room.

We've all done it.

In his book *Gossip: The Untrivial Pursuit*, Joseph Epstein writes,

> I cannot condemn gossip, at any rate not with a good conscience, if only because I enjoy it too heartily, even while I understand that too much of it lowers the tone of any society . . . in which it takes place, not to say often ruins reputations and destroys lives. Yet all my life I have delighted in hearing delicious gossip, and I have also felt the strange but genuine pleasure of passing it along and, on occasion, purveying original gossip.[5]

Epstein owns what so many of us struggle to admit: we like the pleasure of passing on juicy tidbits. It might make us feel important. It might make us feel better about ourselves. It might relieve our boredom. It might help us feel a measure of control in a frustrating situation.

How did we get here? How did we end up with a culture that zealously guards our medical information but just as zealously encourages us to tell others' stories without their permission and to talk about others behind their backs?

And why buck the current cultural trend of gossip and work to develop a personal code of confidentiality? Why swim against a strong tide?

Because confidentiality builds trust, and trust builds relationships. And because God calls us to this countercultural way of living.

A Countercultural Call?

Throughout the Bible God calls those of us who love Him to live in a way that demonstrates our love for Him by loving our neighbors (friends, coworkers, bosses, relatives, actual neighbors). I believe that includes the way we use words to talk about people.

The Bible calls me to love my neighbor with the words I speak and with the words I stifle: "Do not let any unwholesome talk come out of your mouths, but only what is helpful for building others up according to their needs, that it may benefit those who listen" (Ephesians 4:29 NIV).

That's a tall order! But perhaps we introverts have a bit of a home-field advantage on the confidentiality playing field.

As introverts, we often struggle to process quickly, and we struggle to find words to express that processing. Spoken words come hard. What a gift when it comes to practicing confidentiality and avoiding gossip that harms!

But written words, which often come more easily to the introvert, can do just as much damage in breaching confidentiality. I know that all too well.

So, despite a slight introvert advantage in the spoken word category, I know I need to pay attention to my words, especially my written words.

> **Introvert Inclinations**
> Often hesitate to speak until they have time to fully process thoughts internally so that they experience fewer incidents of "foot-in-mouth disease."
> Find joy and comfort in listening.
> Gravitate toward the written word, again often avoiding incidents of "foot-in-mouth disease."

Confidentiality

Ephesians 4:29 helps me think through what to say and what not to say in various situations by asking two questions:

- Do my words offer some *benefit* or *build up* another?
- Do my words directly address another person's *need*?

Do my words offer some benefit or build up another?

Imagine interrupting a lunchtime discussion between two coworkers talking about the personal life of a third coworker. They turn to you and fill you in before you can grab your lunch from the fridge. You didn't really want to hear that tidbit, but now you can't get it out of your head. And worse, every time you see that coworker, you think about that conversation.

Our minds don't have an easily accessible erase button. Words stick in our heads, coloring our opinions and our reactions.

Those lunchtime words did not benefit or build up anyone.

- With just a few words a coworker can pass on information that makes another coworker look incompetent.
- With just a few words an employee can ruin a boss's reputation.
- With just a few words two friends can destroy a relationship that took years to build.
- With just a few words family members can launch a decades-long silent feud.

Or

- With just a few words coworkers can devise a way to help another coworker in a difficult personal situation.
- With just a few words an employee can find a way to praise a boss in front of coworkers.
- With just a few words two friends can agree to talk things through.
- With just a few words family members can try to discuss an issue or at least agree to disagree.

My friend of Polish descent knows so well the pain of words. In the 1970s the prevalence of Polish jokes deeply affected this friend, who had an eleven-letter last name.

> In elementary school, as teachers called everyone alphabetically by their first and last name for attendance, I would cringe while waiting for the teacher to stop and try to sound out my name. Then, in junior high, the intensity of "dumb Polack" jokes by fellow students and even teachers intensified my need to be the smartest in order to prove the stereotype wrong. From gentle ribbing to extreme vulgarity, the derogatory jokes conditioned me to be embarrassed about my heritage. I told my dad that I hated being Polish and wanted to change our family name.[6]

My friend ended up as salutatorian in high school, making almost straight *A*'s, but at what cost to her spirit? What if she had heard words from classmates and teachers that built her up and honored her heritage?

Words can build a reputation, help solve problems, bring health, bring hope, bring reconciliation, bring change. They need not destroy.

Confidentiality

Do my words directly address another person's need?

Author Kathleen Norris uses a term, "holy gossip," that surprised me when I first read it.

> The word [gossip] is related to the word for *godparent*, so it has a holy derivation—I was shocked when I discovered this! The unholy kind of gossip is bad, of course, but I have a healthy respect for holy gossip. . . .
>
> That's when the gossips get busy after church and call around. They get in touch with friends, neighbors, and relatives—does he really want to see people? Or is he too tired? Should I drop in today? That is a good use of gossip.[7]

Ah . . . asking questions, practicing empathy, helping—all focused on the needs of another person and not on my need of wanting to feel better about myself or more important or less frustrated or less bored. And not just talking to fill dead air space or gather juicy, often sad details. This sort of talking—"holy gossip"—leads to action, kind action, action meant to build up, strengthen, support another.

Perhaps holy gossip might also include talking about the wonderful, thoughtful things others do.

What Does Confidentiality Sound Like?

Remember the telephone game? Someone whispers a phrase, such as "I have a great chocolate chip cookie recipe" to the person on his right. That person turns to the person on his right and repeats what he heard. After the phrase has passed through a dozen or so people, the last person states the phrase aloud: "I want your chocolate" or "Eye a great cookie."

Nonsense. Partial truth. Twisted truth.

We do this with information and stories so easily. We hear a great story from a friend, and we want to tell it to someone else, but we improve on it. We make the fish a few inches bigger, the bargain a few dollars cheaper, or the loss even more tragic.

Hard to "tell the truth and only the truth" and not to embellish.

What if we thought of gossip as a virus that needs treatment in order to preserve confidentiality? (And, yes, I did write this chapter during the COVID-19 crisis, so I clearly had viruses and vaccines on my brain.) What if we treated our words, spoken or written, with the SAR vaccine (**S**tick to the facts; **A**void names and juicy tidbits; **R**efuse to speculate)?

Stick to the facts.

Instead of saying (or writing) this.

> I think my friend, Dave, lost his job last week. I heard he didn't even get a severance package. I also heard his kids have health issues. And they probably lost their insurance. Horrible!

What about saying (or writing) this?

> A friend of mine found out yesterday that his company is downsizing and has eliminated his position. He is looking for a job in the field of electrical engineering. I thought maybe you would have some connections.

Avoid names and juicy details.

Instead of saying (or writing) this.

Confidentiality

> My neighbor Rebecca just lost her husband of forty-five years to lung cancer. What a long, painful journey! So many appointments and treatments. After eight weeks on hospice, he just died last Monday. My neighbor hasn't left her house since then. I don't know what she is eating!"

What about saying (or writing) this?

> A person I know just lost a family member to cancer and struggles with grief. I know you also lost someone to cancer. What advice could you give me to help this person I know? What helped you? What didn't help?

Refuse to speculate.

Instead of saying (or writing) this.

> Did you hear about Sylvia? Bless her heart! She just couldn't keep that son of hers in line. I heard he got arrested last night. Probably drug-related.

What about saying (or writing) this?

> A woman in our church has a son in a legal situation. Let's ask God to do His good work in their hearts through this situation, and let's pray for understanding people to help this family.

Sadly, churches can often become a place where gossip, not confidentiality, reigns. We often use prayer requests as a place to pass on gossip.

"Did you hear about Sylvia? Bless her heart..."

Nothing in that pile of words suggests trying to *meet a need* or *benefit* or *build up* someone.

But what if someone shared this information differently by **S**ticking to the facts, **A**voiding juicy details, and **R**efusing to speculate? And what if someone only shared this information with a small handful of people, all of whom have agreed to pray and to help and not to share this request with anyone else?

Confidentiality.

My college roommate and decades-long friend, Jacqui, has served several church congregations with her husband. She often finds herself in the position of trying to help people with various difficult situations.

> I will sometimes start out a session by saying, "I don't need to hear all the details of your sorrow. Please speak so as to guard the reputation of your friend/husband/relative."
>
> And as the session continues, I will often interject with, "Do I need to know this?"
>
> It's difficult to carry all of this information in one's head and not share it with anyone, but I've made it a habit not to share private information that people share with me with anyone—even my husband—unless I get permission from the person.

Interestingly, Jacqui has experienced church communities where confidentiality and genuine concern *do* reign over gossip. She explains:

> If zero gossip is consistently modeled in a congregation, it becomes the new culture. Our past two churches had this built into the DNA before we arrived.
>
> We found that when our two youngest children were in high school, they would tell their stories in such a way that we wouldn't be able to discern who they were talking about. They would refer to "a friend of mine" when they wanted to get advice on how to handle their problems with their classmates. We seriously never told them to relate

Confidentiality

their stories this way. It just happened because of what they saw and heard at church.

Because of this, there was very little "drama" in these churches.[8]

Ah . . . the quiet sound of confidentiality. So different than the pain and confusion that abounds in the following story, also from a church setting:

As the music minister of a church for five years, I made lots of friends with choir members and instrumentalists. I had a few really good friends in the church with whom I cultivated close, confidential relationships.

Then the new pastor and I started dating and got engaged and married over a two-year period. People I thought were my friends were suddenly challenged by my minister's wife role and had different expectations of me now than they did of me as a musician. It was difficult when I realized they were talking behind my back about who I was and how they would relate to me.

One person in particular started questioning my close friends and trying hard to limit my scope of friends. This put my confidants, who sang in my choir and loved me, in a difficult spot. I sadly had to stop speaking confidentially to anyone who attended our church.

I realize that I now stay away from close relationships with church people because of our previous church work. I seek relationships outside of the church so I can develop friends.[9]

My heart ached when I heard this story. Oh, that we would put the SAR vaccine (**S**tick to the facts, **A**void names and juicy details, **R**efuse to speculate) to work in churches and preserve and promote confidential, life-giving friendships!

Practicing Confidentiality with Our Ears?

We introverts have what some writers call "superpowers"—things we tend to do well that can make a huge difference.

Listening certainly tops that list.

Because we introverts have trouble finding words and tend to need to form the words first in our brains before we speak them aloud, we often default to sitting back and listening. Frankly, it takes less effort.

Ironically, when it comes to practicing confidentiality, sitting back and listening can sometimes lead us into compromising situations.

Let's say you sit down to lunch (or a Zoom call) with some coworkers and the topic turns quickly to your boss. "Can you believe that decision she just made? What was she thinking? I hear her job might be on the line now. I'm not surprised. What do you think?"

If you linger in this conversation, you will hear things—opinions, juicy tidbits, speculation—that you can't easily forget. So, do you do the introvert thing and settle in for a good listen (after all, you're not *saying* anything that could hurt someone else)? Or do you speak up and say something and perhaps hurt the feelings of the gossiping coworkers?

You could just gather your lunch and say, "Oops. I've gotta go take a phone call." Or if you're on a Zoom call, you could tease your dog with a favorite toy until he or she barks. You could say, "Oops. I've gotta go walk my dog."

Or you could wait for a pause in the conversation and quietly say, "I just don't think we know all the facts yet. I don't want to speculate. What are you doing for fun this weekend?"

Confidentiality

Or you could interrupt the gossiping speaker. Eek! One of my least favorite things to do.

Interrupting a gossip session doesn't come easily for me. I tend to just walk away. But afterwards I think, *I could have said something*, such as:

- Please, let's not talk about someone who isn't here. I wouldn't want that to happen to me.
- I'm sure we don't know the full story. How was your morning? Busy?
- I hear your frustration, but I don't know enough to say anything that could really help. Could we talk about something else?

Just as I need to walk into a room full of people with a few standard questions in my head (see chapter 3), I also need to keep one or two gossip-deflecting questions in my head and pray for the courage to use them. I so don't like interrupting! But I do like speaking words that "build others up." God calls me to that.

> **Introvert Impediments**
> Can dislike interrupting so much that cutting off a gossip feels impossible.
> Can hide behind the anonymity of social media to create a false, pithy, loud persona.
> Often maintain a critical internal dialogue of self and others.

What to Share or Repost?

One Saturday afternoon I popped on to social media to catch up and discovered a post from a writer that included an excerpt of a message this writer had received from a spiteful reader. I read part of the spiteful message and a few of the colorful comments pointing out the flawed thinking of the angry reader, and I closed my laptop with a sigh.

Why did this particular story need to end up on social media? And why did I feel compelled to read at least part of it?

Not my story!

As introverts, we often feel quite comfortable on social media. We don't have to look anyone in the eyes. We don't have to think on our feet. We can make our quiet voices heard. And sometimes we can feel so at home that we just post whatever pops into our heads.

Could we work to practice confidentiality on social media? What a countercultural concept! And something I believe God calls us to. If confidentiality can make or break relationships in real life certainly it can also make or break relationships in cyberspace.

"Not my story" (NMS) matters on social media just as much as it matters in face-to-face conversations. Perhaps it looks like this on social media:

- I won't post a story from someone else or about someone else without that person's permission. (Not my story.)
- I won't post photos (or tag someone in a photo) without that person's permission. (Not my face.)

And the SAR vaccine matters on social media just as much as it matters in face-to-face conversation. Perhaps it looks like this on social media:

- I won't post, repost, or read items that include unreliable, questionable, unvetted *facts*.

- I won't post, repost, or read items that contain *juicy tidbits* about another person that could damage that person's reputation.
- I won't post, repost, or read items that include *speculation* about situations, political or personal.

In his book *Digital Minimalism* author Cal Newport calls readers to evaluate the addictive nature of social media and rethink the ways they use it. He challenges readers to know the "Why?" behind their social media use rather than just getting sucked into it because of convenience or boredom. He promotes digital minimalism, which he defines as:

> A philosophy of technology use in which you focus your online time on a small number of carefully selected and optimized activities that strongly support things you value, and then happily miss out on everything else.[10]

I wonder if we would gossip less online if we had a clearer grip on our deep values, which brings me back to the words from Ephesians 4:29 (NIV): "Do not let any unwholesome talk come out of your mouths, but only what is helpful for building others up according to their needs, that it may benefit those who listen."

For those of us who love God and seek to live in a way that honors Him and draws others to Him, we must pursue practicing confidentiality by shunning gossip—online and in person.

The Quiet Gift of Confidentiality

This countercultural way of living can make all the difference in developing friendships that thrive. Just ask my friend Peggy:

Five years ago my husband's health began to fail, and I became his caregiver.

I attended two meetings of a nationally organized support group for dementia and came home more frustrated than before I went. I knew this was not for me but that I did need the support of people who were experiencing some of the same difficult things I was facing or that were already happening.

One close friend in my neighborhood said that she and three other women who had very sick husbands were getting together and wondered if I would like to join them. Of course, I wanted to give it a try.

I did not know the other women at all and was a bit apprehensive when I walked in the door. The first thing that was said after introductions was that nothing that was said in the group would be talked about outside of the group, and that has remained the case.

We all became very open over time, telling about intimate details of the decline of our husbands' health as well as some health issues developing in ourselves. Subsequently, two more women have joined the group, and we all feel very close to one another, especially now that three of the husbands have died. We seem to be entering another phase in our relationships.

I feel so lucky to have been invited into the group when I was, and I know that the difficult times each of us have gone through have cemented the friendships we share.[11]

> **Challenge Your Introverted Self**
> Craft your own interrupting-gossip statement. Practice saying it out loud a few times. Imagine saying it in a certain situation at work or out with friends or even around a family dinner table. Ask God to give you wisdom and courage about when to use this statement. Then try it.

Confidentiality

Oh . . . the quiet gift of confidentiality.

In the next chapter we'll take a close look at another friendship-building tool: consistency, not to be confused with perfectionism.

Journaling Questions

1. On a scale of 1 (low) to 10 (high), how do you rate yourself on confidentiality? How does that score compare to a score you would have given yourself ten years ago? Why?
2. Describe a time when a friend breached a confidence by telling something about you to another person (or people)? How did you feel? What did you do? What did you say to your friend? What happened to your friendship?
3. What do you think about striving to avoid ever talking about one person (not present) to another person?
4. How do you respond to the term "holy gossip"? Why? And how do you think faith in God teaches and challenges you in the realm of confidentiality within and also outside the church?
5. Think back on your week. What might you have said differently if you had had the SAR gossip vaccine?
6. As an introvert wanting to forge connections that matter, how might you extend the gift of confidentiality to an acquaintance as a first step toward friendship?

Chapter 8

Consistency

Friendship has far less to do with discovering each other and far more to do with developing the relationship. And to develop something implies a process, which implies time, which implies priority, which implies commitment—which implies some level of consistency.

—Shasta Nelson

It started the year our daughter went to first grade and her brother started fourth grade. It continues still, two decades later.

Friday lunch with my husband.

We landed on it because we didn't have to hire a sitter or pay dinner prices. A frugal date.

But after having lunch every Friday for decades, it has become so much more than just a frugal date. It has become a quiet, joy-filled oasis at the end of every busy week. All the distractions of home disappear—the yard full of weeds, the pet in need of a bath, the dryer that makes squeaky noises, the people needing time and help . . .

Of course, we have missed some Fridays due to illness or travel or last-minute work meetings, but we both try our best to protect this time on our calendars. Still.

I don't know how much money we've spent over the years on Friday lunches (despite using coupons), but I do know that it all went directly into the bank account of building a friendship that has become the foundation of our marriage.

When you sit across the table from someone every Friday for twenty-plus years, you learn how to talk to each other about life—the good and the hard. You learn how to show up even when you're a little bent out of shape and talk through it. You learn to admit when you're worn out and need help. You learn how to listen and encourage and challenge.

Friday lunch communicates, *I value you so much that I want to make you a priority every Friday. I want to see you and hear you and be with just you.*

Connecting with my husband has become an every-Friday habit.

Consistency.

As I've talked with friends about this idea of consistency, I've heard some remarkable, creative stories that reaffirm my hunch that consistency builds friendships in a quiet, thoughtful sort of way—just right for an introvert.

One of those friends, a sister introvert, told me a story that began with a summons to serve on a grand jury once a week for eighteen months.

> Every Wednesday, I commuted over an hour to get to the grand jury. Lawyers from the district attorney's office presented federal cases every Wednesday. These days of testimony were often long and emotionally draining, since we had to hear about some very heinous crimes. (Some cases I wish I could forget.) Many Wednesdays, I found myself on the train home absolutely traumatized by the horrible acts I'd heard about.
>
> My friends Nancy and Bob live close to the train station. We'd met at church years before that and had gotten to know each other. I taught some of their kids in Sunday school. Knowing that I had to commute for jury duty, they

Consistency

invited me to have dinner with their family one Wednesday. That dinner invitation turned into a weekly event that lasted the duration of my term on the grand jury, which turned out to be longer than eighteen months because some cases ran over term.

There were many times when I burst into tears in their presence, shattered by the testimony I'd heard. They didn't ask a lot of questions, since I couldn't share the details because I was a jury member. Instead, they prayed for me and provided a hot meal so I wouldn't have to cook. Best of all, they talked about other things to help take my mind off the dark side of life.

I needed their consistency and their welcoming presence. You see, I live alone. Though I'm a believer in Jesus, going home and facing a dark apartment was hard on Wednesdays. But my friends made sure I wasn't alone. I'm more grateful to them than I can ever express.[1]

Consistency: "agreement or harmony of parts, harmony of conduct or practice with profession."[2] In other words, saying we value something and then showing it through our actions.

So, if we value living connected, how do it we show it through our actions? How can we make friendship-building a habit, in a quiet, thoughtful sort of introverted way, of course?

Habits Fuel Change

Surprisingly, the Old Testament relates a fascinating story about habits (involving vegetables!)—all set against the backdrop of the Middle East in 605 BC.

Daniel, a strong, healthy, good-looking, smart young man, became part of an elite group, trained to serve at the royal palace of Nebuchadnezzar, the King of Babylon.

Living Connected

When offered the rich food and wine from the king's table, he balked and suggested instead a trial diet of vegetables and water for ten days. After the test period, the king compared Daniel (and his three friends) to the other young men in the elite program, and they looked "healthier and better nourished" than the other young men (Daniel 1:15–16).

Veggies won the day! (And yes, I do love veggies!) What an interesting habit choice for a young man who had easy access to all sorts of rich, savory, palace-cooked food.

But there's more . . .

When a new king (Darius) took over the kingdom, Daniel remained in leadership, rising to great heights and inciting the jealousy of other officials: "Then the other administrators and high officers began searching for some fault in the way Daniel was handling government affairs, but they couldn't find anything to criticize or condemn. He was faithful, always responsible, and completely trustworthy. So they concluded, 'Our only chance of finding grounds for accusing Daniel will be in connection with the rules of his religion'" (6:4–5).

People who worked with Daniel knew that he did what he said he would do. They couldn't find "dirt" on him. How unusual—then and now!

Consistency.

These jealous officials set a trap for Daniel. They tricked King Darius into signing a law that stated no one in the land could pray to anyone except the king on punishment of death. These officials knew that Daniel had a habit of praying to God, three times a day. And they knew him to be a man who stuck to his habits.

Daniel prayed to God anyway: "But when Daniel learned that the law had been signed, he went home

Consistency

and knelt down as usual in his upstairs room, with its windows open toward Jerusalem. He prayed three times a day, just as he had always done, giving thanks to his God" (6:10).

Daniel just kept doing what he always did—kneeling in prayer. Clearly, that habit of prayer, in a humble posture toward God, shaped both his private and public persona.

A habit.

Start Small

Experts argue over how long it takes to make an action a habit and thus enact a true change. Some say thirty days. Others believe a new habit takes three months to take root. James Clear, author of *Atomic Habits: An Easy & Proven Way to Build Good Habits & Break Bad Ones*, says it takes sixty-six days for a new behavior to become automatic.[3]

Hmm . . . sixty-six days.

James Clear has made the study and execution of habits his life work. It started with his own battle to overcome a coma-inducing baseball injury as a high school student. In addition to weightlifting and exercising regularly, Clear also focused on getting good sleep and keeping his room tidy! He went on to become a top athlete at Denison University and then a best-selling author.

Clear presents a compelling case for *atomic habits*—"a regular practice or routine that is not only small and easy to do, but also the source of incredible power; a component of the system of compound growth."[4] In other words, "a little habit that is part of a large system."[5]

So, let's apply this to friendship. If we want to develop friendships (our "large system"), then how do we nurture little habits that will help us find and cultivate friends?

If we follow Clear's way of thinking, we do NOT attempt an instant and intense revamp of our lives and ourselves in order to become more likeable. We can take building friendships, introvert-style, one small (consistent) habit at a time, starting with prayer.

- Maybe we designate certain days to pray for coworkers.
- Or we make it a point to pray for neighbors every weekend.
- Or we pray daily for our boss.

What about a weekly email to a friend or small group of family members? A "Sunday hello" email? We introverts gravitate toward the written word, making emails and texts a good way for us to connect.

My friend Anna reminded me of another way to develop a simple, small friendship-building habit. She said, "I have known Jean since high school. We have consistently communicated even over distances of one, two, or four thousand miles for over four decades. During the past ten years, we have enjoyed a one-hour phone call scheduled every other month on the first or second Sunday at a consistent time, convenient to both of us, as we now reside two time zones away."[6]

Granted, we introverts don't love phone calls, but scheduling it like an appointment makes it more manageable. (And our extroverted friends so enjoy a phone call.)

Author James Clear also has a fabulous, simple idea for creating new habits, something he calls habit-stacking: "One of the best ways to build a new habit

Consistency

is to identify a current habit you already do each day and then stack your new behavior on top."[7]

If we apply this principle to building the habit of prayer into friendship, it might mean:

- When the alarm goes off in the morning, also set a reminder to go off on your phone to pray for coworkers.
- When you pass your neighbors' houses on a walk or drive on the weekend, make it a point to pray for them.
- As your computer boots up every morning, pray for your boss.

Other small "habit stacks" might include:

- When you brush your teeth every morning, think of one person for whom you feel grateful. Determine to send that person a text after your stash your toothbrush: "Just saying hi" or "Thinking about you."
- When you sit down to eat lunch, look through your email contact list and send out one email to say, "How are you today?"
- When you log out of your computer for the day, say goodnight to one coworker. You can come up with a few stock phrases: "Thanks for the day;" "Have a good one;" "Nice seeing you today."

Nothing huge. Nothing loud. Just consistently reaching for other people but doing it in a way that suits our introverted selves.

> **Introvert Inclinations**
> Often feel more comfortable with predictable schedules and plans.
> Can find creative ways to communicate consistency without saying anything out loud.
> Tend naturally to put pieces together and analyze what worked well and what went wrong.

Cultivate the Big Habit of Showing Up

These little habits begin to add up and help us work toward that "larger system" of cultivating friendship.

They also give us fuel to begin to cultivate the big habit of showing up. By that I mean showing up in the real world—the world beyond prayer, texts, emails, and social media.

Showing up in real life feels daunting for an introvert. It feels loud and noisy and unpredictable.

But it has to happen at some point.

Many years ago John commented on my affinity for books. He once looked at the books on the shelves (and the floor) of my office and said something like, "Wow! You have a lot of books!"

I nodded and smiled. "They are my friends."

John laughed and said, "Nobody needs that many friends."

Truthfully, hanging out with book friends comes easier for me than hanging out with flesh-and-blood friends. Friendships in real life get messy and complicated and frustrating.

But I also know the joy and strength such relationships bring. I've seen it in my own life over and over.

As I began to work on this book, I also began to meet with four other women writers of faith, part of the Redbud Writers Guild. We agreed to meet the sec-

Consistency

ond Tuesday of every month at a local restaurant. We also agreed to divide up the tasks we needed to keep our group running. We even signed a covenant agreement. We kept at it for six months.

We spent time listening to one another and praying for one another, and we read each other's words and offered encouragement and suggestions. We began to trust one another and build friendships.

And we watched books take shape—four of them. All because we showed up. Every second Tuesday. And several of us claimed the title of *introvert*.

Way back in the 1970s, long before the words *spiritual direction* and *mentoring* became part of our everyday vocabulary and thinking, the author Alan Loy McGinnis (*The Friendship Factor*) told a remarkable story.

> I meet with a group of seven men every fortnight who talk about our thoughts and feelings and then pray for one another. These men are all strong leaders—pastors of large churches or bold, aggressive doctors. When people such as these meet regularly, month in and month out, a certain amount of competitiveness is inevitable, and we sometimes grate on one another's nerves.
>
> One man, a very successful scientist and physician, possesses by far the strongest intellect among us and finds it easy to grab the conversation and run off on hobby horses without considering the others. Since the purpose of our meeting is not to discuss intellectual issues, my friend routinely gets tackled when he is about five minutes into these monologues and barely warmed up. At times we have been so hard on him that I have felt guilty when the meeting was over and wondered if he would be back.
>
> But here is a wonderful thing—the man never stays away because we have been critical. Doubtless he would just as soon find something else to do some weeks, but he is a man who abides by his commitments. He had made a pact with us that we would link arms and support one another

as Christian brothers, and though at times the relationships have produced sparks, he has not flinched nor fled.

The result? That man is a fast friend to each of us, and there is little that we would not do for him. He says now that he has never had companionship such as the seven of us enjoy together, that we are his best friends. And he is right—we love him dearly and perhaps are all the more loyal to him because of the way he has weathered our beatings, listened to our reactions, and worked the complicated connections through.[8]

Cultivating the big habit of showing up acts as a powerful friendship-building tool between people who mutually agree to meet consistently.

A writer-friend, Jenny, told me a delightful story of how what started as a job turned into a surprising friendship.

> I was ushered past the bustle of the senior living center entrance and brought into Charlotte's nicely sunned room where she sat dozing. Her daughter-in-law gently jostled her awake.
>
> Charlotte's daughter-in-law had called the graduate school at which I was a student and employee and declared to my supervisor that she needed someone to spend time with her mother-in-law. After a pleasant interview with her family, I was brought one day to meet Charlotte to see what she would think of me.
>
> Charlotte looked me over thoroughly that day with a clever and kind gaze. I discovered that she was educated, shrewd, sharp-witted, and humorous. She was also well-read and easily conversant. At the end of our time, she turned to her daughter-in-law and declared, "I like her. She speaks in full sentences with correct grammar. And we've already found we share a love for British literature and theatre. She and I should get on royally."
>
> And so I collected Charlotte each Friday morning and planned an interesting outing for the day, always including

Consistency

a fine place for lunch after which she had a standing appointment at the Neiman Marcus's salon for her hair setting, manicure, and chin waxing. Our jaunt would end with my drive to the grocery store to select her groceries while she accompanied me by wheelchair.

She introduced me to another world, as if time had rewound to 1942. Charlotte was a self-made woman, survivor of the Depression, college-educated in the 1930s, and left widowed at forty to raise her young children.

For five short hours of my week, I delighted in her humor, her historical commentaries, her dialogue, and the strands of poetry she would quote. She was kind and curt, fiery and frail.

We had fifteen short months together before she died. Despite our sixty-year age disparity and the business arrangement that instigated our meeting, we became friends. She became closer to me in one way than even my own grandmothers.

Our times together taught me that meaningful connection can happen between any two who try.[9]

As challenging as it feels to get ourselves out the door, clearly friendship only develops and grows when we keep showing up. In real life.

I've watched with joy as my husband has discovered the gift of showing up.

I met Stephen a few years after college, almost forty years ago. We both attended the same church in New Jersey and lived close enough to one another that we could get together regularly. I found him to be tremendously smart, insightful, godly, and just fun to be around. When I got engaged several years after meeting him, I asked him to be one of the groomsmen.

But then life took over for both of us, as it does—busy jobs, young kids, and limited vacation time. I had moved to the Midwest. Frequent phone calls turned into occasional emails, and then eventually into just an annual Christmas card.

Then in 2013 I traveled east to see family and got together with Stephen. After a great couple of days together, we each said, "Hey, let's do this again." But without a plan, I knew we were both going to settle back into our busy lives a thousand miles apart, and another twenty years could slip by.

I suggested we set a schedule. Once every May, I would visit Stephen on the East Coast for a weekend. And in November he would come see me in Chicago.

This changed everything. Having a date meant we could look forward to it and schedule other things around it. We would reschedule if something came up for one of us, just as we would for any other appointment. The regularity of our get-togethers has served to elevate our friendship and been tremendously life-giving. All we needed was a consistent plan.[10]

We introverts may not find travel quite as energizing as my extroverted husband does, but we certainly can find ways to show up for people in quiet, thoughtful sorts of ways. We can't let fear win and just stay home all the time.

Do Not Let Fear Win

Let's push pause for a minute and talk about the fears we introverts often battle that keep us from showing up in real life: fear of rejection, fear of imperfection, fear of the unknown.

We fear rejection.

What if I work hard to show up for a potential friend over a period of months, even years, but ultimately that person decides I just don't make the cut as a friend? What if he or she stops showing up and maybe even says, "I just don't think we have what it takes to be friends"?

All that time wasted! And oh, the aching heart!

But also what an opportunity to learn. What went wrong? Why? Did I miss red flags? What would I do differently next time? What would I do the same the next time? How can I find the strength to cultivate another friendship?

We may also fear imperfection.

What if I can't do friendship the way I think (or read) that I should? It all can feel so complicated and daunting. Why bother? Especially when I clearly know my weaknesses and limitations.

If only we could remember that everyone has imperfections and give ourselves some slack. If only we could say, "I'm flawed, but that does not disqualify me from friendship."

We fear the unknown.

What if I work really hard at connecting to a person and then that person moves away or gets terminally ill or has a drastic, personality-changing, midlife crisis?

Living through a pandemic has shown me in living color that even if we prepare and think and plan, life still unfolds in unexpected, often painful ways. We can rage against it, try to control it, try to escape from it . . . Or we can trust ourselves enough to have the inner strength and faith to face what will come, knowing that change and challenge will shape us in good ways if we let them.

These very real fears can paralyze us if we let them. They can also prompt us to make some creative excuses about why we can't commit to showing up.

> **Introvert Impediments**
> Can feel so comfortable at home that leaving home creates fear.
> Can overanalyze self and dwell on mistakes, creating self-doubt.
> Can easily employ their creative brains to invent myriad creative excuses not to go out.

"So sorry, I can't make it. I have a tight work deadline."
Work always makes for an excuse not to connect with people socially. But if we view connecting as a top priority, it should often win out against work deadlines and maybe even force us to become more scheduled. I know that if I truly want to attend an event and connect with people, I can plan around a writing project.

"So sorry, I can't make it. We have a family situation going on right now."
Families always have situations going on. Hard to argue with a crisis. But we all know that while some situations do need our immediate attention, others can wait an hour or two. Solving a crisis or meeting a need can feel so much safer to an introvert than walking into an unknown situation with people.

"So sorry, I can't make it. I need to be home for my kids."
Kids certainly need parents who help them, but

> they do NOT need parents who hide behind them. Kids need to see parents who step into challenge, especially the challenge of connecting with others. They need to see parents who say, *This feels hard and scary, but I know it matters so I will do it.*
>
> **"So sorry, I can't make it. I double-booked myself."** What if consistently showing up mattered so much that we carefully scheduled and protected our times with people? What if we kept a calendar (paper and/or electronic), set reminder alarms, and worked hard not to overcommit by giving ourselves twenty-four hours to think, pray, and talk to wise counsel before we say yes to any new commitment?

May we learn to recognize fear and excuses and push back against them as we pursue living intentionally as connected, introverted people.

Live Intentionally

I never thought about creating a personal mission statement until I attended a StoryBrand conference, led by writer Donald Miller.

The older I get, the more I realize that it makes sense to aim at something rather than just let life push and pull me.

At the StoryBrand conference, Miller presented his Productivity Schedule.[11] I use it almost every day and find that it helps me lay out projects for the day, but it also helps me figure out why I want to do these projects by including a blank space at the bottom of the sheet that reads, "My Life Theme."

As part of the StoryBrand conference, Miller emphasized words he wanted to define himself, such as *humble* and *hospitable*. He urged us to do that too, using the Productivity Schedule as a helpful tool.

By developing a life theme and writing it and/or posting it somewhere I frequent daily (my planner and my computer), I have a much greater chance of living consistently and reaching the target for which I am aiming. I evaluate and tweak my Life Theme once a year. For now, I aim for this target:

> As a Jesus-loving introvert who seeks to live connected, I will intentionally practice approachability, generosity, honesty, hospitality, and humility.

Take a moment now to think about your own life theme. (Question 7 below will help you do that.)

I hope to look back on my life and feel and see a thread running through it that stitches together a lifetime of connections into a large, cozy quilt called friendship.

Peggy, a master quilter, describes the making of friendships beautifully.

> For forty-one years I have been a member of a very small group of women who quilt. We meet every two weeks and have taken many field trips to quilt shows and museums over the years. We have opened our doors to women new to town and needing a group of like-minded quilters to join.
>
> The membership has evolved over the years as people move away or die, but I have remained in close touch with the ones who now live elsewhere as well as the ones who remain in this city.
>
> We have all improved at our craft over the years and the longtime friendships mean that we can critique and give advice on each other's work without hurt feelings.

> We also revel in sharing the joys of marriages of our children, the births of grandchildren, birthdays, and so on. By this time, we have all become so comfortable with each other that we pretty much know what to expect from each other. This is a cozy aspect of longtime friendships.
>
> Quilting brought us together all those years ago. I doubt I would have met any of these women otherwise. I count them as my most cherished of friends.[12]

May we embrace and practice the friendship-building tool of consistency.

May we also have the wisdom to know when we have become stuck in our ways, enmeshed in rigid routines that no longer grow friendships. May we have the wisdom to know when flexibility should triumph over consistency, something we'll talk about in the next chapter.

> **Challenge Your Introverted Self**
> Who in your life would you like to get to know better? How could you show up consistently in this person's life for the next month, indicating your interest in creating a friendship? Bonus points if you do it mostly in real life.

Journaling Questions

1. How would you rate yourself as a consistent friend on a scale of 1 to 10, 1 being not at all consistent and 10 being highly consistent? Why?
2. What does the story of Daniel say to you about habits?
3. What friendship-building habits do you already pursue? How have they helped you live connected?

4. How could you develop a friendship-building habit or two or three by using the technique of "habit-stacking"?
5. Think about a time when you showed up for someone, or when someone else showed up for you, over a period of weeks or months. What happened to your relationship? What happened in your heart?
6. Describe a time when you let fear (of rejection or inadequacy or perfection or the unknown) keep you from showing up for someone. How do you wish you had handled the situation?
7. Take a few minutes to look back at previous chapters. As an introvert, which words do you want to define your relationships? Begin to craft your own Life Theme:
   As an introvert, I will

_____

_____

_____

_____

Chapter 9

Flexibility

Emotionally agile people are dynamic. They demonstrate flexibility in dealing with our fast-changing, complex world.

—Susan David

Almost every weekday morning for ten years, between 7:30 and 8:15, my phone whistled at me with a text, zinging from my across-the-street neighbor's house. She has a dog (Chase) and I did too. We all loved to walk in the morning.

> **Bev:** Walk at 7:50?
> **Afton:** Yes!

Some days I might have already gone to work or one of us might have had a slow start after a sleepless night.

> **Bev:** Walk at 7:50?
> **Afton:** Not a chance, sorry. Moving extremely slow this morning!

Living Connected

Bev did not get bent out of shape if I could not get moving fast enough to keep her dog from driving her crazy. She just took a walk. I did the same.

> **Bev:** 7:50?
> **Afton:** Slow moving, may be ok with 8.
> **Bev:** Ok. Text when ready.
> **Bev:** Someone is driving me crazy. We need to go now. Hope we catch you.[1]

If I had proposed to Bev: "Let's walk every morning at 8," I don't know if it would have worked. Dogs have minds and opinions and bladders of their own. And sometimes one of the four of us just needed a slower morning.

I suppose Bev and I became *flexibly consistent*. We showed up for each other consistently but on a flexible schedule. And now that Ringo, my sweet cockapoo, has died, Bev and I keep practicing flexibility to find times to see each other a few mornings every week. That first walk without Ringo made both our hearts ache.

Frankly, the word *flexibility* ("the ability to bend easily or without breaking"[2]) scares me. As an introvert, I like to plan ahead and schedule events so I have time to prepare. Because I don't think or talk well on my feet, flexibility can and usually does force me to walk into uncomfortable situations.

And yet, I know from experience that practicing flexibility *does* build friendships. Ringo and Chase showed me that.

That term *flexibly consistent* gives me hope. We will explore it in this chapter as we seek to answer the question, *How can we introverts learn to practice flexibility but also stay true to ourselves?*

> **Introvert Inclinations**
> Prefer time to process information and situations rather than act in the moment.
> Prefer time to prepare for social situations by thinking and developing questions.
> Need rest and time to refuel with quiet after engaging socially.

Why Does Flexibility Matter?

Before we settle in to talk about how flexibility matters in relationships, let's also take a quick look at how it matters in terms of physical and mental health.

Harvard Medical School explained the importance of physical flexibility this way: "A well-stretched muscle more easily achieves its full range of motion. This improves athletic performance—imagine an easier, less restricted golf swing or tennis serve—and functional abilities, such as reaching, bending, or stooping during daily tasks."[3]

I discovered firsthand the pain of not having full range of motion with my shoulder muscles when I developed frozen shoulder. I couldn't reach above my head or behind my back. Physical therapists and a chiropractor taught me stretching exercises that eventually helped my shoulder unfreeze. Now I know that I need to keep doing those exercises, especially when I feel a twinge in my shoulder. I want to maintain full range of motion with my muscles.

I also want to maintain full range of motion with my friendships. I don't want to get stuck in patterns that shrink my world or my connections. I know that I need to keep stretching and practicing flexibility, all in a quiet, thoughtful way of course.

And I also know that for the sake of my mental health, I need to work at practicing emotional flexibility.

We introverts, who spend so much time in our heads, can easily get sucked down rabbit holes of shame from the past or worry about the future. Licensed clinical psychologist Chris R. Mazzarella borrows a phrase from Dr. Joe Dispenza, the *generous present moment*, to describe a practice of engaging fully in the moment rather than getting stuck in the shame of the past or anxiety about the future.

He explains: "Most people have tens of thousands of thoughts a day, with most of those thoughts being the same as yesterday. We're following our programming. When we learn to live in the generous present moment, we accept that all possibilities are available to us in the present and step away from that programming."[4]

Working to live in the *generous present moment* can help us get out of our heads, fight depression, and reach toward the people in our lives instead of staying caught in loops of shame and worry.

Embracing the *generous present moment* helps us stay emotionally flexible and therefore more open to life and to connecting with others.

Author Shasta Nelson uses the metaphor of bamboo to create a visual picture of flexibility at work in relationships: "Bamboo bends with the wind, never fighting against it. But it doesn't blow away with the wind, it stays rooted. Its ability to bend without breaking or being uprooted is so beautiful. It's the perfect metaphor for flexibility—being able to go-with-the-flow without ever losing our center or our roots."[5]

Flexibility

So how do we introverts stay true, stay rooted, to our quiet souls yet also embrace flexibility?

What Scares You?

Scrolling through Facebook one day, I came across some posts from a writer-friend—posts that still ring in my head because they gave me courage. Melody posted about owning her introversion while traveling, something that does not come easily for me. I asked her to tell me more.

> I've had a passion for travel since I was young. I knew I would go places and see the world . . . and by God's grace, I have seen four of the seven continents. And the desire to see more of this beautiful planet continues to grow inside of me.
>
> Traveling while honoring my gifting and wiring as an introvert, however, has been a journey for me that's developed with grace and priceless insights over time.
>
> Once I began to understand who I was as an introvert and how my introversion shows up in my travels, I was able to create the type of space and bandwidth I needed to properly care for myself.
>
> For example, before work trips, whether they are conferences where I'll be around fifty or hundreds of people, or writing assignments that will take me around the world, I take a day or two before those trips to rest, pack, prepare, and have solo time alone to charge up. I also take two days off to rest and recharge and have solo time alone when I return from those trips.
>
> I believe the best gift I can give myself as an introvert when traveling is to know how to use this strength well during travels and also how to care for this part of my being.
>
> Simple things help, like paying a little extra for early bird check-in for some airlines so that I have my spot secured in line and don't have to rush "trying to get in where

I fit in." I am a tall woman so paying a little extra for seats on some airlines that provide more leg room also helps me care more for myself. I travel with ear plugs and ear buds to help me cancel out noise that can be overwhelming and drain my energy as an introvert.

If traveling with others, I tell them what I might need, in terms of solo time, to support my introversion so I can show up well in our interactions. My explanation helps my traveling companions understand I'm not being distant or antisocial. Communication is key with others.

During my travels, I also seek out ways to have solo time to help me recharge. This is one of the crucial things I've learned about my introversion: I must have time alone so that I can rest and replenish my energy. Traveling can take a lot from my energy reserves, from constant movement to meeting and speaking with new people to navigating new cultures abroad. Solo time helps me care for myself deeply, which then supports me well in how I show up in the world and engage with others.

I do my best to think about what I need and what will care for me best before I travel and also make space to give myself grace and compassion when there are unexpected things on my trips, and I need to use intellectual and emotional flexibility in the moment to respond. I can't plan for everything. But I can decide how I will respond to what comes my way and learn from those experiences.

Learning and understanding introversion—that it is a gift and unique set of wiring for people—helped me grow in how to take better care of myself in this area.

Introversion is not a weakness. It is a strength.[6]

What courage and hope Melody's story gives me to work at staying flexible to new experiences and people while also owning my title of *introvert*.

Her story points me back to that phrase *flexibly consistent*. Melody remains consistent with herself by honoring and respecting her needs as an introvert, but

Flexibility

she also practices flexibility by opening herself to new experiences.

Many years ago, I came across a quotation that challenged me: "Do one thing every day that scares you." Lots of people attribute the quotation to Eleanor Roosevelt, but it actually came from *Chicago Tribune* columnist Mary Schmich in her address to the graduating class of 1997.[7]

When I discovered the quotation, I had long ago graduated from college. In fact, I faced a newly empty nest and a lot of time at home alone, trying to work as a freelance writer and editor. For the first time in a very long time, I could structure my days as I wished. An introvert's dream!

But into that oasis of quiet crept fear and self-doubt. My world began to shrink, month by month.

I began to ask myself, *Did God call me to this, or have I chosen isolation?*

After months of praying and talking to wise friends, I realized that I needed to heed Schmich's advice. I needed to do something that scared me. I needed to open a door and trust God to use a new experience to teach and change me and help me live connected, not isolated.

For me that meant getting a job that took me outside my house. I needed the challenge of showing up regularly, learning something new, and navigating relationships with coworkers. I knew that I could all too easily back out of a volunteer position, so I knew I needed a job with a contract and people who counted on my showing up consistently.

And I wanted to see what would happen within me if I stepped out and tried something different. I wanted to give God the chance to show up in new ways. I wanted to try on flexibility. (Please know that in all this talk about doing things that scare us, I do *not* advocate embracing a dangerous or abusive work or home situation.)

I did eventually get a job in a field I knew very little about: healthcare. And, oh the things my introverted self has learned, especially about interacting with people.

So what scares you, especially as an introvert? And what do you do about it? Run? Hide? Just "buck up and do it"? And what do you do when life takes unpredictable turns?

How Do You Handle Curveballs?

Nothing like living in a pandemic to force the issue of flexibility.

Overnight people went from working in office buildings to working at home, often surrounded by children who suddenly had to learn online.

College students left for spring break, expecting to return to campus and to a celebratory graduation ceremony. Instead, they returned home and never had the chance for goodbye hugs.

Essential workers still went to work and had to navigate anxiety and ever-changing protocols.

Businesses had to close and then reopen and reconfigure.

And then, just when we felt like we could breathe again and start to resume normal life at least a little, we hit the winter surge of 2020. We watched and waited and wondered if lockdowns would happen again.

So much up in the air! *So* much possibility of change without warning. One tiny virus managed to throw the entire world a curveball.

Flexibility

We all reacted to this differently. Some days (if we could even separate one day from the next) we felt overwhelmed. Other days we reacted to everything with irritation. Anger and blame won the day. I often found myself longing for a schedule again.

Reading these words from psychologist Susan David helped me:

> Emotionally agile people . . . are able to tolerate high levels of stress and to endure setbacks, while remaining engaged, open, and receptive. They understand that life isn't always easy, but they continue to act according to their most cherished values and pursue their big, long-term goals. They still experience feelings of anger, sadness, and so on—who doesn't?—but they face these with curiosity, self-compassion, and acceptance. And rather than letting these feelings derail them, emotionally agile people effectively turn themselves—warts and all—toward their loftiest ambitions.[8]

As I read Susan David's words, I thought about one of my most cherished values: connecting with people. Sending emails and texts works to an extent, but in the new, socially distanced, COVID-19 world, I felt like I just needed *more* to forge the real connections I so value.

So, I pushed myself to do something that scares me, something many introverts abhor: making phone calls. But I did it introvert-style. I set up the calls ahead of time so I would have time to prepare a quiet place to talk and think of topics to discuss. I often walked while I talked. And after every call, I took time to think back over the call and let it go.

Some people developed new hobbies during the pandemic: painting, cooking, writing, drawing, sewing, quilting, hair-cutting . . .

I learned to talk on the phone. Ta-da!

That doesn't mean I also became an extrovert. It just means that I worked at something that scares me because my people matter deeply to me and (go figure!) some of them *love* to talk on the phone.

> **Introvert Impediments**
> Can find phone calls frustrating.
> Can feel overloaded by too much stimuli, including a noisy room, back-to-back conversations, and myriad details.
> Can bend too much to accommodate other, louder voices.

If we want to build friendships, we do have to stretch ourselves to practice flexibility in communication, but we introverts can still do that in a quiet, thoughtful sort of way.

Flexibly consistent.

Just as this pandemic craziness began, a friend of mine found herself in the middle of her own sort of crazy. She needed surgery and then rehab at a facility. When she returned home, she faced lockdown as well as mobility issues and pain. After several long, challenging months, she learned that she now had an infection and would need two more surgeries, followed by more months of immobility and multiple stays in rehab facilities.

So many twists and turns. And all on top of the recent death of her husband of more than fifty years.

My friend could have whined and complained and yelled. She could have shut herself down and cut off friends and treated herself to a good, year-long wallow. But she didn't. She understood that she couldn't change the circumstances and situations, and so she adjusted—practiced flexibility.

Flexibility

As I watched and listened and learned, I saw my friend navigate the curveballs of her life with humor and style, steeped in faith, and surrounded by friends.

Flexibility.

Life, whether mid-pandemic or post-pandemic, throws us curveballs. And how we respond or don't respond can so deeply affect those around us.

One of my sisters-in-law, Ellen, told me about a phrase she has used for decades, a phrase that developed from getting sick on her honeymoon.

> Back then they still served dinners on airplanes. I discovered some red stuff halfway through my chicken dinner and realized it wasn't completely cooked. I didn't think too much about it until I threw up later all over a sidewalk on the Mexican island where we had just arrived. And then I spent the next few days heaving over a toilet. My new husband, Tom, was fine—he had ordered the beef.
>
> We chose this honeymoon spot because some good friends of ours had gone there the year before us. They told us it was warm and reasonably priced but not glamorous. I think they were afraid we wouldn't like it. I remember one of them saying, "The main thing is you'll be together."
>
> That phrase stuck in my mind as I kept throwing up. Tom and I started using it with each other: "The main thing is we're together."
>
> After three days of being violently ill, I recovered and we enjoyed snorkeling, riding mopeds, and going to local markets.
>
> I often remember that trip now when I make plans with someone, and we have to change them because of the weather (or a virus). Or when something I planned or cooked doesn't turn out as fun or delicious for everyone as I had hoped. Things happen.[9]

Perhaps many of us will adopt this phrase, or some variation of it, after having spent so much time away from one another during the pandemic. Maybe we will care a bit less that everything looks and tastes perfect and care a bit more that we can actually gather together inside and hug each other again.

"At least we're together!"

Can You Bend Too Far?

Sometimes we introverts can let our voice get lost in the din of others' voices. We let others pick the restaurant. We let others decide how best to celebrate life milestones. We let those with stronger opinions tell us at length what they think we should think about the current political situation.

We bend and bend and bend.

We become so flexible that we no longer live consistently as ourselves. We lose our voice—literally and figuratively.

For introverts this can mean that we try to bend *ourselves* to navigate events ("just suck it up and act like an extrovert!") instead of letting ourselves bend the *event* to better suit our quiet souls.

Consider these ways to bend the *event*, not yourself.

- "I'll go with you to the party, but I want to drive myself there so I can leave before the drinking starts and things get really loud."
- "I'd love to have dinner with you, but could we pick a quiet restaurant or pick up food and eat at my house?"
- "I'm sorry, but I just can't go out with you tonight because the stimulating conversation will keep me up late, and I have to get up early for work tomorrow. Could we get together on a

Flexibility

night when I don't have to work the next day? Or get together for breakfast or lunch?"
- "Thanks for the offer to eat lunch together in the break room, but I just need to catch my breath today over lunch and eat in the quiet of my car. How about we meet before work tomorrow and take a walk together?"
- "I'll drive myself to the meeting. It helps me to have the quiet time in my car to think and prepare."
- "I would enjoy a getaway weekend with friends, but I'll navigate it better if I have my own room."
- "I would like to hang out with you today, but I also need some time to myself at the beginning and end of the day."
- "I would like to get to know our neighbors too, but could we invite them over one family at a time for a backyard dessert."
- "Having family here for Thanksgiving sounds fun, but could we plan some events for the afternoon and have some questions ready to discuss over the meal?"

All voices matter in relationships. And we introverts can find ways to own our quiet voice yet still connect with others.

If we don't manage to practice *flexible consistency*, we could find ourselves in a lot of frustrating, awkward situations like this one:

> I was the leader of a small group and had someone in my group who was new in town. I really wanted to reach out to her.
>
> I found myself sitting with her watching some weird alien movie she wanted to see. And we even ended up at

a country music concert where she sang along to all the songs.

I was frustrated. We really had almost no interests in common.

Eventually, I discovered that what worked best for us was to get together with our kids.

I don't regret making the effort to connect with this woman, but I realize now that I needed to find things to do together that we *both* enjoyed.[10]

Interesting that sometimes practicing flexibility in a relationship means saying "no" or "yes, but." Other times it means stretching to say "yes."

Ah, the friendship dance of knowing when and how to bend.

My friend Sharla, an introvert, describes it this way:

> During my homeschooling years, time with friends was built into my routine. Every week we met other homeschool families for swimming lessons, science co-ops, writing clubs, and other classes. These wonderful activities not only gave my children opportunities to learn and grow, but they gave *me* time with other homeschool moms. While we watched the kids swim in the pool or dissect a frog, we swapped joys and struggles of parenting and teaching.
>
> When my kids outgrew those activities, my scheduled time with friends also disappeared. New routines took the place of homeschooling events: writing in the morning, teaching piano in the afternoon. I love having a consistent rhythm to my day, but neither of those activities fueled my need for friendship. Typing at the computer meant time alone. Teaching young students eighth notes and treble clefs offered interaction with people, but it wasn't the same as spending time with a friend.
>
> As time went on, I noticed loneliness and isolation creeping into my life and so I made a decision. Even though

Flexibility

I love my introvert routines, I promised myself that if someone called me up and asked me to meet for lunch or coffee, I would say yes if at all possible.

I will always love my routines as a means to work consistently, but at this stage in my life I know I also need to practice flexibility to build relationships.[11]

So why bother trying to practice flexibility as a friendship-building tool? Why not just say to people, "I'm an introvert so I don't do small talk or phone calls or big events"?

Because God asks us to live connected, even as introverts.

> **Challenge Your Introverted Self**
> Think of one thing that scares your introverted self but matters to someone you love (talking on the phone, going to large gatherings). Write down the reasons this one thing scares you. Now write down why it matters to your loved one. At the bottom of both lists, write, "I will embrace flexibility by taking one step this month to face this situation that scares me." And then write down one thing you will do. Just one thing.

What Fuels Flexibility?

In my twenties, I often said aloud, "I can't wait to be sixty!" At the time, life felt rather precarious and unpredictable. Would I find a job I really liked that paid me enough to support myself? Would I learn how to make lifelong friends? Would I marry and have a family? I thought that certainly by sixty I would have answers to those questions. Life would have become predictable. Ah! And I have always loved predictability. Not so much flexibility.

Sometime during my twenties, I latched on to the biblical story of Abram/Abraham.

> The LORD had said to Abram, "Go from your country, your people and your father's household to the land I will show you.
>
> "I will make you into a great nation,
> and I will bless you;
> I will make your name great,
> and you will be a blessing. . . ."
>
> So Abram went, as the LORD had told him; and Lot went with him. Abram was seventy-five years old when he set out from Haran. (Genesis 12:1–4 NIV)

The words "So Abram went" leapt off the page for me. God called Abram to go, and Abram went. Just like that! He didn't drag his feet. He didn't come up with a million excuses for needing to stay close to family and what he knew. He went.

Talk about flexibility!

Hebrews 11:8–10 (NIV) gives us a glimpse into why Abram (later renamed Abraham) could find the courage to uproot his entire life.

> By faith Abraham, when called to go to a place he would later receive as his inheritance, obeyed and went, even though he did not know where he was going. By faith he made his home in the promised land like a stranger in a foreign country; he lived in tents, as did Isaac and Jacob, who were heirs with him of the same promise. For he was looking forward to the city with foundations, whose architect and builder is God.

By faith.

Flexibility

Abraham had great trust in God. He knew that if God asked him to travel, God would go with him and provide for him at each step. And he knew that God would honor him for listening and obeying. That faith bred confidence. And flexibility.

We who seek to love Jesus can have a similar confidence, even we introverts. When God calls us to live connected, even practice flexibility in that process, we can know that He goes with us in that journey. He equips, encourages, and provides.

Sharon Garlough Brown's book, *Sensible Shoes*, tells a delightful story of flexibility, of growing in faith by learning to stay open to God's direction.

One of Garlough's characters—petite, silver-haired retreat and spiritual director Katherine Rhodes—explains:

> Self-examination isn't about being perfect. It's about listening and responding to the Spirit. It's about allowing God to reveal where we are hiding and resisting his love so that we can come out from hiding to receive grace and mercy and wholeness. This isn't about beating ourselves up, and it's not an invitation to obsessive introspection. We can't make ourselves whole or holy. That's the Spirit's work. Our work is simply to cooperate with the Spirit by saying yes to God's movement in our lives.[12]

So what does saying yes to God look like in your life in terms of living connected as an introvert?

To what or to whom do you need to say a resounding "Yes"?

To what or to whom do you need to say a "Yes, but could we change something"?

To what or to whom do you need to say a firm "No," standing up for your own quiet voice?

Take some time now with the journaling questions to mull over this concept of flexibility as a friendship-building tool. And then join me in the next chapter for a look at another way to grow friendships: creativity.

Journaling Questions

1. On a scale of 1 (low) to 10 (high), how would you rate your flexibility in both the physical realm and in the emotional realm? Why?
2. What do you struggle with most in terms of relational flexibility? Why?
3. As an introvert, how do you respond to that word *flexibility*?
4. What scares you in terms of relating to people? Why? What keeps you from addressing this fear? How might you take one tiny step toward addressing this fear?
5. Describe a time when you bent too far in a relationship. What happened within you? What happened to the relationship?
6. How have you found ways to live *flexibly consistent* as a connected introvert?
7. How has your faith in God given you flexibility fuel for relationships? Or how might you begin to let your faith grow your flexibility in this area?

Chapter 10

Creativity

I don't ever want to stop growing, being creative.
—Luci Shaw

Did you know that donkeys have the power to craft a friendship? Suzanne explains it beautifully in this story.

> When our sons were all grown up and moved out, my husband, Randy, and I found ourselves restless and living with two dogs in a condo in downtown Madison, Wisconsin. After searching for several years, we finally found our dream farm. I'd been keeping three horses at a boarding facility and looked forward to bringing them home to live with us on our own farm. Only one thing was missing: a donkey. I'd wanted one for years, pointing out to anyone who asked why they could be calming to a herd of horses and fun for our granddaughter and other children who visited the farm.
>
> One afternoon I sat down at my computer and, as I'd done many times before, typed *donkey* into the search engine. Among the pictures that came up this time was one of a sad-looking, eight-year-old donkey available for adoption at a sanctuary not far from Madison. That donkey immediately set up residence in my heart, and I needed to go meet him.
>
> Now, I have many friends who are experienced with equids who would have loved to meet that donkey with me and offer their advice, but I invited my friend Lori instead, and fortunately she agreed.

Living Connected

Randy and I had met Lori and her husband, Marc, a couple of years earlier when we started attending the church where Marc is lead pastor. As soon as we met Lori, we knew she was special and deeply loved by her family and friends. And we soon learned that her gracious and calm nature belies an adventurous spirit and an unusual appreciation of cold weather! Truly, I felt blessed to hop into my truck with Lori for the ninety-minute drive to meet the lonely donkey.

When we arrived at the donkey sanctuary, we were cheerfully greeted by a petite woman named Angela, who oversees the entire operation. She led us to the sad donkey and told us what little she knew about his history: that he'd spent most of his life alone, had been surrendered when his owners were getting divorced, and had endured some unknown duration of neglect. Furthermore, his years of being alone had apparently impaired his ability to form connections with other animals and humans. In fact, he'd been adopted out twice already and returned each time because of his inability to bond with animals or humans.

As if to confirm what Angela was saying, the donkey dodged every gentle effort Lori and I made to engage him. Sadly, he didn't seem like the best donkey for the job I had in mind, a donkey that would bond with horses and enjoy the attention of children.

So Angela introduced us to a pair of miniature donkeys. These two were playful and interactive, and it was easier to picture them bonding with the humans and horses on our farm.

On the way home, Lori and I chatted nonstop about the donkeys, and I could tell she was as hooked as I was. But it was the lonely donkey that had our hearts. With our collective mothering experiences combined with her years of teaching middle schoolers and mine as a physician, we brilliantly concluded that he needed special care.

We wondered, for example, was there such a thing as an autistic donkey, or was he depressed? Clearly, he needed another chance at life, but what could we do for him that hadn't already been tried? Then it came to us—what if we

Creativity

gave him all the time he needed to adjust, even if it took years, and what if we adopted the happy miniatures also, so he'd have donkey companions?

It seemed like a good plan, but how, I wondered aloud, would I explain to my husband that my quest to rescue one donkey had turned into a quest to adopt three donkeys? Lori said she'd back me, which is what friends are expected to say at times like this. Turns out, she was sincere.

As soon as we got home, I excitedly explained to my husband our logic for adopting three donkeys instead of one. He looked perplexed so I explained again, and maybe once or twice again, and two weeks later we became the proud parents of three rescue donkeys that our granddaughter named Anna, Elsa, and Sven.

Lori and I began meeting weekly to handle, groom, and train the donkeys. Often other people joined us, adults and kids alike. Over many months we saw Sven's confidence grow. He began to bray when he saw us approaching, to make eye contact, and to move with better posture and balance.

Lori and I learned a lot about donkeys and were pleasantly surprised that we could apply these lessons elsewhere in our lives. And while caring for and playing with the donkeys we had opportunities to talk about other things in life, to lean on and encourage one another, and to laugh and cry without getting too silly or sappy.

When you spend time with donkeys, other people can tell. There is a faint "donkey aroma" you can pick up with your nose. As I've gotten to know Lori, I've discovered that she has an "aroma" too, one that comes from spending time with the Lord and in community with other believers. Aroma may be a weird way to say it—it's not actually something you smell with your nose, but it's a good way to explain that there is a sense you get about a person who has recently spent time with the Lord and others who love Him.

The pandemic has put a temporary halt on our getting together in person, but Lori and I talk easily by phone. I know the Lord has plans for us and am humbled and grateful to be continuously reminded that we can bless others, including animals, by remaining open to adventures, no matter how small or insignificant they may seem.[1]

Suzanne and Lori, both quiet souls, took the risk of trying something new and consistently showing up for each other—and for Sven, Elsa, and Anna. And they crafted a friendship woven together with donkey stories: "Remember when you first got Sven?" or "Remember the first time we tried to ride Sven?"

Imagine how our relationships might come to life if we bathed them regularly in large doses of creativity. What if we, like Suzanne, reached out to a potential friend and said, "Would you like to join me in a painting class, a long-distance bike ride, a cooking class, a garden walk, a book club . . .?"

Creativity—a breath of fresh air, a new perspective, an outside-of-the-box approach.

Luci Shaw, a prolific author and poet, describes creativity this way: "The creative impulse is essentially innovative. It's always discovering new areas to explore. It experiments. It breaks down old barriers and ventures into unknown territory. That implies a kind of risk."[2]

What might happen in our relationships if we invited creativity into them, especially with the idea of creating friendship stories?

Build Friendship Stories through Shared Creative Pursuits

Who of us does not love a good story?

"A long time ago in a galaxy far, far away . . ."[3]

Creativity

Or "This is the story of a man, one who was never at a loss. He had travelled far in the world, after the sack of Troy."[4]

We grew up hearing stories, studying stories, writing stories. Story surrounds us.

In a delightful book, *Leap Over a Wall*, author Eugene Peterson, a master storyteller, explains the power of story: "Story is the most adequate way we have of accounting for our lives, noticing the obscure details that turn out to be pivotal, appreciating the subtle accents of color and form and scent that give texture to our actions and feelings, giving coherence to our meetings and relationships in work and family, finding our precise place in the neighborhood and in history."[5]

So how can we creatively develop our friendship stories?

We can look for others who share our creative passions.

I recently discovered a delightful book, *A Year Between Friends 3191 Miles Apart: Crafts, Recipes, Letter, and Stories*, which chronicles a friendship that first began online.

Two photographers, Maria Alexandra Vettese and Stephanie Congdon Barnes, found each other on Flickr, a photo management and sharing application. One December day in 2006 they both posted photos that echoed each other. That prompted them to start a yearlong conversation with each other from their homes 3,191 miles apart. Stephanie lives in Oregon; Maria lives in Maine. And in 2016 they collaborated on a book that oozes with craft ideas, photos of everyday life, short letters, and recipes. The string of a growing friendship ties them all together.[6]

These photographers remind me that social media can become a friendship-making tool as people with common interests find each other and even find the joy of collaboration.

I love the connection I have on Facebook with the other women of faith in the Redbud Writers Guild. We celebrate writing milestones, pray for each other as life happens and deadlines loom, share expertise about social media, platform-building, book launches . . . I can talk about the nitty-gritty bits of the writing life with these women, a language and a world all its own.

Because writing requires great gulps of solitude, I find that staying connected with sister Redbuds pulls me back into the world of people and brings me balance and perspective. How nice to know I don't have to know everything about the writing life; I can ask a sister Redbud. And we can collaborate, just as photographers Vettese and Barnes did.

Perhaps you love native plants, woodworking, dogs, model railroads, baseball, true crime podcasts, jewelry making, studying foreign languages, or WWII stories. Perhaps you know someone who might enjoy learning with you more about these interests.

> **Introvert Inclinations**
> Tend to have creative imaginations that help them envision a finished project.
> Often enjoy hands-on activities, such as painting, woodworking, drawing, cooking, and sewing
> Often have great powers of concentration that enable persistence with a creative endeavor.

Creativity

We can try something new. Together.

Jayne Wilson Bowman reminds me of the joy of creating something with a friend. She helps run a busy family business, Homeland Creamery, in Julian, North Carolina.[7] Days at Homeland Creamery start early and end late with everyone pitching in to help create ice cream flavors, such as Cupcake, Lemon Crunch, and Orange Creamsicle. Their dairy products have become well-known throughout North Carolina.

In the midst of such a busy life, Jayne told me that she discovered a creative way to stay in touch with Sharon, her best friend in high school. They tried something new to both of them.

> Sharon and I like the same kind of things. She is a no-frills, laid-back sort of person. What you see is what you get. I like that. She has three kids and two grandkids and lives about forty minutes away from me.
>
> We lost touch a bit after high school, but one day I discovered a brochure about this basket-making class at the Liberty Artisan and Craft Gallery in Liberty, NC, and sent it to her.
>
> We decided to do a day-long event, called "A Weave In." We got breakfast, picked out a basket we wanted to make, worked on it, then had lunch and worked on another basket. All those jokes about basket-weaving aren't true—it's really hard on your fingers, especially if you don't have the right tools, which we didn't the first time.
>
> Later we also took a class and made a child's rocking chair. That was really fun.
>
> Making baskets and a chair with Sharon gave us a great time to talk and catch up.
>
> And it was good for me to get away from the daily pressures of the creamery.[8]

I've heard stories of friends enjoying extreme sports, taking all-day hikes, stamping homemade cards, fishing, taking cooking classes, learning to make pottery, organizing book clubs, hunting for bargains at thrift stores, learning to play musical instruments, serving at a food pantry, working at an animal shelter, creating a podcast, developing a blog, training for a marathon, and many more.

We can communicate creatively.

My husband loves the creativity involved with texting. He routinely sends wacky photos, silly songs, *Seinfeld* clips, YouTube videos, and greetings in a foreign language (through Google Translate). His texts provide much humor, but they also communicate with joy, "Just thinking about you!" John's texting habits remind me not to get stuck in a rut and to stick to just communicating information!

In college I had a quirky habit of stuffing notes inside books. I love returning to some of those books decades later and finding a note from a family member or a friend or a former professor. Perhaps you know a book lover who would enjoy opening a volume to discover a little note from you.

What about sending old-fashioned letters and notes that require a stamp?

We can share a common, household task.

I have discovered that a lot of relationship-building happens around the creative task of cooking.

During my senior year in college, I lived in an apartment with three women, all of whom I had first met on my floor freshman year: Jacqui, Jody, and Linda.

Creativity

When we moved into our apartment, Linda suggested we name it. In deference to her Italian heritage, she suggested Bella Casa Mia (my beautiful home). It stuck.

These three women brought with them to the Bella Casa Mia (BCM) a love of cooking. We decided to divide up nights and assign cooking/dishwashing partners. And we all agreed to fling wide the BCM doors and invite professors, friends, staff, and family members for dinner.

This way of living felt natural to two of my friends; they had grown up around tables buzzing with food and discussion. I had not. I watched and learned as we had multiple dinner guests each week. What a marvel to see firsthand that food could create such connection.

As our senior year came to an end, we decided to try and capture a bit of the BCM for all of us to take with us as we scattered across the country, so we created a cookbook of our favorite recipes. Jacqui handwrote them in her lovely script. I supplied the literary quotes. Jody supplied the verses of Scripture. Linda helped run copies on the mimeograph machine and punch holes in the pages. We all strung the pages together with yarn.

We each kept a copy of our BCM cookbook, but we also made extras and gave them to some of the people we had invited for dinner and other friends and family members.

As I look back on it now, forty-plus years later, I realize that not a lot of graduating college seniors would feel compelled to compile a cookbook. But we *had* to do it. What better way to celebrate the story of our year together—a story of connection based on cooking.

In the years after college, I often turned to Jacqui's Dutch Baby recipe or Jody's Strawberry Pretzel Salad recipe or Linda's Apple Brownie recipe. I did it partly because I loved the recipes but also partly because I loved my friends. As I cooked, I remembered them. And thanked God for that year of cooking we shared as college seniors. And for the lifelong gift of these three women who remain the dearest of friends, committed to their marriages, families, friends, and especially to a deep, life-sustaining faith in God.

As our fiftieth birthdays rolled around, Linda's oldest daughter, Kate, graduated from our alma mater. I knew I wanted to do something special. I returned to the story we four women had told our senior year—our cooking story. I put together a typed and bound version of our BCM cookbook. Of course!

After many years of use, my original BCM cookbook had become torn and stained. I knew I needed to preserve this BCM cookbook, this visual representation of the cooking story we wove together. On days when I felt lonely, discouraged, and disconnected, I knew I would want to pull out this book, cook something, and then text one of my friends, "I just made your stroganoff for dinner! Thinking about you."

Our cooking story.

You might find joy in creating a paint-a-room story, a putting-together-furniture story, a grocery-shopping story, or even a power-washing story that involves neighbors.

Learn from God through Story

I love that God chose to speak to us through the creative genre of story. He knew that these stories would nurture and challenge us in ways that reading lists of

Creativity

rules and commands would not. I find that I return again and again to some biblical stories and find something new and life-giving in them with each reading. I can't tell you how many times I've read the stories of the prodigal son (Luke 15) and King Jehoshaphat (2 Chronicles 20). I also find myself drawn to the friendship story of Ruth and Naomi (as told in the Book of Ruth).

The story begins with Elimelech and his wife, Naomi, a Jewish couple who lived in Bethlehem with their two sons, Mahlon and Kilion. When famine hit, the family decided to relocate to Moab, a country with more food but also a country hostile to Jewish people.

Elimelech died in Moab, leaving Naomi as a widow with two sons. Eventually, the sons married Moabite women, but then ten years later, the sons also died. Lots of loss and sorrow. Layer upon layer of it.

Naomi made a bold decision and gathered her two widowed daughters-in-law, Orpah and Naomi, to head back to her homeland where the famine had ended. Shortly into their journey, Naomi encouraged the two younger women to stop traveling with her and go back to their own mothers. Orpah, through many tears, sadly left, but Ruth adamantly refused to leave Naomi.

> But Ruth said, "Don't force me to leave you; don't make me go home. Where you go, I go; and where you live, I'll live. Your people are my people, your God is my god; where you die, I'll die, and that's where I'll be buried, so help me GOD—not even death itself is going to come between us!"
>
> When Naomi saw that Ruth had her heart set on going with her, she gave in. And so the two of them traveled on together to Bethlehem. (Ruth 1:16–19 MSG)

Apparently, Ruth and her mother-in-law had crafted a deep connection to each other while living in Moab, despite their cultural differences. Perhaps Ruth had worked hard over the years to help her mother-in-law adjust to a foreign culture. Perhaps they had bonded in part over their mutual loss. Clearly, Ruth had observed Naomi's life-sustaining faith in God, through times of joy and times of sorrow, and taken on that faith herself.

Ruth and Naomi wove their lives together in a story of connection that involved cross-cultural challenges, loss, faith, a road trip, and eventually romance and joy. (Don't miss the end of the story in Ruth 4.)

This story draws me in again and again every time I read it. This friendship story crosses cultural and age boundaries and portrays a friendship between in-laws, all undergirded with a deep faith in God.

Sounds a lot like "[breaking] down old barriers and [venturing] into unknown territory"—Luci Shaw's definition of creativity.[9]

Ruth and Naomi certainly stepped into a friendship experiment, breaking down cultural barriers and venturing into new territory together—literally and figuratively.

Their story illustrates in living color the joy of taking the risk of friendships with in-laws, people in an older or a younger generation, and people of other cultures. The joy of living and seeing creatively.

Connect Creatively with In-Laws

We don't choose our families, especially our in-laws. And we don't have to see them a lot if we so choose, simply navigating a relationship of civility on holidays.

Creativity

But what if, like Naomi and Ruth, we could use creativity to develop life-giving friendship with in-laws?

My husband loves to walk, and he loves cities, particularly New York. The buzz of the city suits his extroverted personality.

I've accompanied John on a few walk-the-city escapades and realized that I just don't enjoy it the way he does. I would rather take a long walk alone or with one person in the countryside. As Susan Cain says, "Introverts feel 'just right' with less stimulation."[10] So I've encouraged John to do his walk-the-city adventures with friends who enjoy them more than I do.

As I write this chapter, John has started a conversation with two of his brothers-in-law about getting together for a weekend in Chicago. I smile as he recounts the emails and texts flying about the weekend. And I remember that I want to plan a quiet weekend with two of my sisters-in-law.

Often family gatherings can feel overwhelming for an introvert because of all the buzz and activity. But what about balancing that buzz with some one-on-one activities? Cooking together before the big family gathering? Cleaning the dishes together after the big dinner? Asking someone, an in-law perhaps, to take a long walk after dinner?

> **Introvert Impediments**
> Tend not to think well on their feet so may feel uncomfortable with spur-of-the-moment creative, unplanned activities.
> Love deep conversation so much that they can forget the joy of *doing* things with others.
> Find creative group endeavors frustrating, preferring one-on-one interaction.

How can you creatively make time to know better the people in your family, especially the in-laws?

And what about reaching for friendship across generations?

Connect Creatively across Generations

The story of Naomi and Ruth also shows a beautiful story of cross-generational respect. They learned from each other and supported each other in hard times and in good times.

Every day when I walk into my home office, I glance at a handmade piece of pottery—a flowered, yellow watering can. It has a permanent spot of honor on my filing cabinet because I need to remember the giver of this gift as I sit down to write: Professor Helen de Vette.

Professor de Vette's college creative writing class lit a fire within me to rediscover words. She did it by teaching techniques and pointing me to great works of literature, but she also did it by offering genuine words of encouragement.

When she retired and I graduated, I expected to lose this connection of professor and student. I did not anticipate Professor de Vette's efforts to stay connected.

We often bumped into each other at college literature conferences since we both lived near the college. Then she invited me to stop by her welcoming, green house one afternoon to have tea and talk about words and writing. I left her house grinning and refreshed, dosed in the scent of words. And determined to return often.

Our word story.

Creativity

As she aged, Helen (at some point, we shifted to using first names) began to ask for help. Could I help her lead a journaling class for other college women? Could I drive her to the women's luncheon at the college?

And now I had the chance to encourage *her*—to remind her that her *words* still mattered to me and to many others.

When Helen left this world for the next, I knew that I still needed to surround myself with her encouragement. I needed to remember her voice, "You can write!" The pottery watering can she gave me years ago says it to me now every day.

Perhaps you have experienced the joy of intergenerational friendship. I hope so. If not, how might you creatively seek to connect with someone of another generation? A coworker? A neighbor? A former professor or teacher?

And, if you find yourself in that "older generation" category, how might you make yourself available to someone of a different generation?

And what about creatively and intentionally pursuing cross-cultural relationships?

Connect Creatively across Cultures

We don't know the private discussions that Naomi and Ruth had with each other, but I would imagine that some of them had to do with cultural issues: *Why do you do things this way in Moab?* or *I don't understand this way of doing things in Bethlehem.*

They allowed their differences to grow them together, not apart. And they grew in their respect for each other.

In her thoughtful book, *Invited: The Power of Hospitality in an Age of Loneliness*, author Leslie Verner writes about reaching for people across cultures, whether living in Uganda, China, Chicago, or Colorado.

> I didn't even realize I had a culture until I lived with a Ugandan family for six months during my senior year of college. Like air, breathing, economic security, and health, I took my culture for granted until I was no longer surrounded by it. Away from my Western culture, I gasped for breath, astounded that every rule I had considered to be universal had shifted. Body language, vocabulary, attitude, daily rituals, social expectations, and even what was considered "biblical" all carried mysterious underlying assumptions that I scrambled to decode. I felt as if I were walking on the ceiling and lying down on the walls.[11]

Verner remembered how it felt to live in another culture once she returned to the States after also living in China for five years. She intentionally pursued friendship with international students, often welcoming them into her home, helping them navigate language and cultural issues.

She inspires me to keep my eyes and ears and heart open for ways to practice creativity with people of other cultures, to "break down old barriers and venture into unknown territory" as Luci Shaw says when talking about creativity.

Author Sheila Wise Rowe says it so clearly in her book *Healing Racial Trauma: The Road to Resilience*: "When we are at our best, we are different people groups existing in the same space while continually learning how to get along and having constructive conversations about making our lives and this country better for everyone."[12]

How might you creatively pursue a cross-cultural connection, in a quiet, thoughtful way, of course?

Creativity

Creativity helps us look for friends in unusual places, and it also breathes life and humor and joy into our existing friendships, helping us develop friendship stories.

What friendship stories do you want to develop? Perhaps one of them has to do with hospitality, something we'll discuss in the next chapter.

> **Challenge Your Introverted Self**
> Think about some of the creative ideas you have rolling around in your head. Take one of these ideas and develop a plan to share it with a friend or friend-to-be. How might your friend collaborate with you on the project?

Journaling Questions

1. How do you define creativity?
2. On a scale of 1 (low) to 10 (high) how would you rate your current friendships on a creativity scale? Why?
3. How does the story of Ruth and Naomi speak to you about friendship?
4. Have you experienced friendship with an in-law? If so, what did you find life-giving about it? If you have not experienced this, what kept you from pursuing connection?
5. Have you experienced a cross-cultural friendship? If so, what did you find life-giving about it? If you have not experienced this, what kept you from pursuing connection?
6. Have you experienced a intergenerational friendship? If so, what did you find life-giving

about it? If you have not experienced this, what kept you from pursuing connection?
7. In ten years, what story would you like to have built with a friend? What one step can you take this month toward crafting that story?

Chapter 11

Hospitality

Friendship grows best in intentionality, and hospitality is the warmest kind of intentionality there is.
—Janice Peterson

I will always remember a particular visit to my great-aunt and great-uncle's cottage on Long Island Sound during my young adult years. They have five children who also have children and some even have grandchildren. I don't remember how many of them piled onto the porch that particular afternoon. I settled in to enjoy the buzz of conversations, but I also felt a bit lost. I didn't know these relatives well, certainly not as well as they knew one another. And as an introvert, I didn't really know how to enter their conversation.

Not long into our visit, my great-aunt Barbara slipped quietly into the seat next to me on the porch and touched my arm. In her quiet, kind way she asked me a question or two and helped me ease into the family conversation.

I remember that kind gesture every time I find myself in a large gathering. I try to do what my great-aunt Barbara did for me—I scan the room and look for a quiet soul who could use a word of encouragement. I know how it feels to have someone notice you and draw you into a conversation.

I also know many people struggle alone with walking into a room full of people. A writing friend and sister introvert, Nilwona Nowlin, told me about her struggle when trying to find her way in a room: "If I'm one of the only people of color in a space, such as in a business meeting, around a table at a conference, or in a classroom, I already know people are questioning if I'm qualified. I feel the pressure to speak up and go against who I am as an introvert."

Nilwona went on to explain some creative ways she copes in such situations: "I've learned to deal with a situation, such as when discussion begins in a classroom, by knowing what I want to say and speaking first. In a work situation, I try to offer a spark of an idea by being the first person to speak. I frequently say, 'This is just off the top of my head, just my initial thoughts.'"[1]

I never thought of Nilwona's approach of taking the initiative. No wonder she has inspired many through her workshops on introverted leadership.

Her story also makes me wonder what would have happened if someone in her space, at a conference or in a classroom, had quietly taken the seat next to Nilwona and said, "I'm so glad you're here" and then asked a simple question, such as "What interests you about this topic?"

Taking initiative. Noticing. Hospitality.

Author Janice Peterson describes hospitality this way: "the welcoming reception and treatment of guests and strangers in a warm, friendly, generous way."[2] In a delightful video, you can see this played out as Janice and her husband, Eugene, welcome Bono to their house in Montana. Bono had come that day to talk with Eugene about his translation of the Psalms (https://www.youtube.com/watch?v=-140S5e90KY).[3]

As we take a look at the many ways hospitality can grow friendships, we'll certainly talk about ways to

Hospitality

practice hospitality at home, but we'll also take a close look at out-of-the-house hospitality.

Stretch for Hospitality

Perhaps some of us come equipped with a hospitality gene, but I would guess most of us do not. It takes effort, thought, and time to reach out to others, especially for introverts. Reading a book often sounds more life-giving. Why not just say, *I'm an introvert. I don't do hospitality?*

Because of Jesus. He reminds me so clearly: "And you must love the LORD your God with all your heart, all your soul, all your mind, and all your strength. The second is equally important: 'Love your neighbor as yourself.' No other commandment is greater than these" (Mark 12:30–31).

I can't really love my neighbors (coworkers, extended family, friends) if I don't ever physically interact with them.

A biblical story, found in 1 Kings 17:8–16, gives me wisdom and courage to stretch myself and offer hospitality.

> Then the LORD said to Elijah, "Go and live in the village of Zarephath, near the city of Sidon. I have instructed a widow there to feed you."
>
> So he went to Zarephath. As he arrived at the gates of the village, he saw a widow gathering sticks, and he asked her, "Would you please bring me a little water in a cup?" As she was going to get it, he called to her, "Bring me a bite of bread, too."
>
> But she said, "I swear by the LORD your God that I don't have a single piece of bread in the house. And I have only a handful of flour left in the jar and a little cooking oil in the bottom of the jug. I was just gathering a few sticks to cook this last meal, and then my son and I will die."

> But Elijah said to her, "Don't be afraid! Go ahead and do just what you've said, but make a little bread for me first. Then use what's left to prepare a meal for yourself and your son. For this is what the LORD, the God of Israel, says: There will always be flour and olive oil left in your containers until the time when the LORD sends rain and the crops grow again!"
>
> So she did as Elijah said, and she and Elijah and her family continued to eat for many days. There was always enough flour and olive oil left in the containers, just as the LORD had promised through Elijah.

Interesting that God chose a poor widow to help the prophet Elijah. Why choose someone already stretched so thin? Why not choose a wealthy farmer?

Clearly God wanted to provide for Elijah, but it seems He also wanted to provide for the widow and her son. And that provision came all wrapped up in sharing food, an act of hospitality.

Why?

Perhaps this widow needed the visual, daily reminder that when you honor God and love the people He brings across your path, you will always have enough. Enough food. Enough time. Enough energy.

She gave. And she received.

I hang on to this story. As an introvert, I often feel I don't have "enough" for hospitality—enough time, enough conversational skills, enough ability to juggle many things at the same time, enough ability to think on my feet and crack a funny joke.

But in this story, I see God asking this widow to offer what she had, however meager.

How I need to remember this! I can so easily get caught up in feeling the need to provide "perfect" hospitality. And that utterly wears me out.

Hospitality

Shun Perfection

I have had a lifelong battle with trying to do hospitality at home perfectly. I've spent so much mental and physical energy on planning menus and cleaning. I guess the cleaning and preparing give me a measure of control.

John and I once invited several neighbors over for dinner. I planned to make homemade pizza and homemade ice cream, both fairly easy. But I did *not* plan on getting a tooth pulled that morning. While waiting in the endodontist's office, I texted a neighbor and told her the situation. She offered to help. I told her I thought I could still do it.

I arrived home after the tooth extraction and started to work on dinner. The ice cream was already made. My mouth kept bleeding. I sucked on some tea bags and sat down. And wrapped an ice pack around my head.

At any point, I could have said to a neighbor or to John, "Let's just order pizza." I didn't. I had in my mind this delightful time of conversation around the table with homemade pizzas. I could do it!

Neighbors arrived. The pizzas came out of the oven, and I sat down at the table with a mouth that still ached and still bled. Half an hour into the evening, I excused myself and went to another room with my ice pack.

So much for great conversation around the table! I had utterly worn myself out. My bleeding mouth told the story.

What if I had said to myself and others, "I had an unexpected challenge today. We're ordering pizza. What would you like?"

I keep trying to let go of this need to do it all perfectly.

Maybe part of my desire for perfection comes from my introversion and not thinking well on my feet. Hospitality holds so many unexpected surprises; I tell myself that if I prepare well, I can react better to surprises.

Maybe.

Or maybe I have confused entertaining with hospitality. Author Jen Schmidt explains the difference this way:

> The entertaining host seeks to elevate herself. . . . When the guest arrives, the entertainer announces, "Here I am. Come into my beautiful abode and have the honor of partaking of all the wonderful things I've spent hours getting done for you. . . ."
>
> Hospitality is different. . . . It transforms our selfish motives and elevates our guest. When the hospitable hostess swings wide the door, all her attention focuses outward: "You're here! I've been waiting for you. No one is more important today than you, and I'm thrilled you've come."[4]

Tom, my brother-in-law, told me a story that speaks to the power of practicing hospitality rather than entertaining.

> Back in the 1970s, hospitality in my house meant setting the table in the dining room instead of the kitchen because company was coming over for dinner. In 2016 my wife and I had to devise a different approach. I had a new coworker who moved from London to our city for the job. We wanted to welcome Havah and her husband by having them over for dinner, but we didn't know how—Eli and Havah are both Modern Orthodox Jews and very observant of kosher.
>
> I asked Havah if there was a way we could do it. She was thrilled at the invitation and said, "Instead of dinner, let's just make it bring-your-own-snacks."

They came, we all clicked immediately with laughs and hugs, and together we spread out our munchies and fruit for a great evening together. It was clear a friendship was born.

Over the next two years, we did lots of things together, and the friendships grew deeper around discussions of culture, sports, spirituality, and international politics. And we laughed a lot!

In 2018, an unexpected family situation required Eli and Havah to move back to Tel Aviv where Eli grew up. Nevertheless, we have all stayed in frequent contact online, plus Havah still works for my company, which involves regular interaction professionally.

In 2019 we visited them in Tel Aviv for several days, including an unforgettable Shabbat evening dinner with Eli's parents and siblings. In 2020 Eli and Havah were back in the US for three weeks, and we met again for a couple of days together.

Who knows what's next, but it's pretty incredible how a simple bring-your-own-snacks evening turned into a four-way hospitality of sharing our lives with one another as friends.[5]

I continue to learn that hospitality doesn't depend on delicious food or a beautiful, clean setting. And I continue to try some hacks that make hospitality at home easier for me.

Try These Hospitality Hacks for Introverts

Inviting people over for dinner (or snacks) takes effort and at least some planning. It can feel so much easier to avoid hospitality altogether and just leave it up to the extroverts.

But we introverts actually have a hospitality advantage; we know how to listen, and we like doing it! A listening ear definitely provides a warm welcome, the heart of hospitality.

> **Introvert Inclinations**
> Often have creative reservoirs full of ideas,
>   including how to connect with people.
> Understand the gift of noticing another,
>   especially a quiet soul.
> Like having a role, such as host.

So how can we offer hospitality at home, introvert-style?

Keep it simple.

Instead of planning an elaborate meal and cooking something you've never made before, come up with three or four go-to dinner menus and stick with the known. Any guest in my house has probably had Hechto's chicken (named for my friend Karyn Hecht, who gave me the recipe), lasagna (with no-cook noodles), chicken potpie, homemade pizza, or Belgian waffles. I've made them often enough that I don't stress myself out knowing if they'll turn out.

I might invite guests for an outdoor dessert on my porch. Or a cup of coffee on the way to an appointment.

Keep it small.

We introverts get easily lost in a crowd, even in our own houses. And we love conversations that go beyond the details of life and work and family. A small group of two to four people makes deep, honest conversation much easier.

Keep questions ready.

In chapter 4 I wrote about the wooden box of questions we keep on our dining room table. This has fostered so many memorable conversations. You may not want an actual box, but you can come up with several standard questions to keep in your head. Questions offer everyone time and space to talk.

Keep it purposeful.

Because we introverts like to "go deep," passing food around a table and making small talk can feel trivial. Many introverts I know have discovered that offering hospitality with a purpose makes all the difference.

Dorothy Greco, a writing friend, explains it this way:

> I'm a highly sensitive introvert who can easily feel overwhelmed or impatient in meandering social events. I love people, but I don't love small talk or party games. Because my husband is a pastor, and we both lead in a local church, opting out of socializing is not an option. Over the years, I've discovered that inviting church friends over for dinner and engaging in meaningful conversation energizes me and helps me stay connected.
>
> We tend to be fifteen to twenty years older than most of the people we partner with or lead. That means we often serve as mentors. Though there's obviously a place for formal, structured teaching in church settings, I believe that the best mentoring takes place informally. We will sit around our table, passing food and talking about everything from how to recognize and handle transference with a team member to how to get teething babies to sleep. No subject is off-limits.
>
> Over the last twenty-five years, we've broken bread with hundreds of mentees. We've taught them how to recruit volunteers, structure teachings, and establish boundaries. We've prayed, wept, and celebrated with them—and along the way, developed deep friendships. By simply making a meal and opening up our home, we help them to feel loved and supported. Because these occasions are focused and missional, I rarely feel overwhelmed or at a loss for words. In fact, I often talk more than my exceedingly extroverted husband![6]

Keep at it with a friend.

My question-loving, extroverted husband loves practicing hospitality. Because we've come to an understanding of our personality differences, I happily prepare the food and orchestrate the behind-the-scenes details while he helps guide the conversation. Often, we do talk ahead of time about some possible questions, and I remind him to notice the introverts. That doesn't mean, however, that I can zone out and not participate in conversation. I have to remind myself to listen *and* talk.

Keep in touch with your people-fatigue meter.

I often imagine a meter on my emotional tank. Does it register 100 percent, 40 percent, 5 percent? The more I've learned to do this, the more I realize when I have reached or exceeded my capacity for interaction. I need quiet to refuel. Sometimes a situation demands ignoring that meter and simply pressing on to help, but for the most part, that meter needs tending. I continue to learn that when I feel this way, I need time to take long gulps of quiet. That might mean slipping away for a bathroom break or heading to the kitchen alone to make coffee and get dessert ready.

> **Introvert Impediments**
> Struggle with small talk around a table.
> Become physically drained after intense conversations and connection.
> Need quiet before and after events, especially those hosted at own home.

Hospitality

I love how another writer-friend JoHannah Reardon owned her introverted personality and learned her limits with hospitality, including telling extroverted friends, "I have to have an hour before bedtime to wind down." If friends tried to stay longer, JoHannah learned to say gently, "It's been lovely, but I've got to get some rest."[7]

Keep trying.

Like anything, practicing hospitality again and again makes it easier.

Surprisingly, hospitality has become one of my great joys. During these days of COVID-19, I often walk by my dining room chairs and sigh. *When will they contain people?* Stretching myself to "Love my neighbor as myself" has led to so many life-changing conversations and friendships, many of them around our dining room table.

We've welcomed neighbors there, college students, nieces and nephews, family members, local friends, and friends passing through on their way to another destination.

Over and over God has shown me that when I stretch and reach for others by extending hospitality, I have enough—enough food, enough time, enough energy.

I know that when we step out of this pandemic, I will need to keep reminding myself to offer a warm welcome rather than focus on perfection. Remembering my lunch with Willow will help.

One pre-COVID-19 day, I invited my friend Willow for lunch. Some of my favorite recipes come from her. She loves to cook and has a fabulous garden where she grows much of what she cooks.

I followed my own advice and made chicken potpie for lunch. But then, I decided to whip out my new Instant Pot and try a dessert I had spotted in my new cookbook: Molten Lava Cake. Perfect! The day before our lunch, I set out to cook the dessert in cute little pottery cups and tried to follow the directions. Alas, I discovered a runny interior. Sigh! I put the cakes in the oven and cooked them until a toothpick inserted in the top came out clean.

Willow arrived the next day, and we settled in for food and conversation in my sunny dining room full of Norwegian knickknacks.

Then I served dessert.

We each picked up a fork and pierced the top of a cake. Oh my! I felt as if I were trying to cut through rock. And when I finally did get a bite on my fork, it tasted a bit like chocolate sawdust. We both kept trying for a few more bites, and then just burst into bellyaching laughter.

I explained my cooking procedure to Willow mid-laugh, and she said softly, "Isn't the point of Molten Lava Cake that it is runny inside?"

Oh . . .

When Willow left my house that day, I thought, *That was fun! Certainly not perfect, but fun!*

I keep learning by doing that hospitality depends more on a warm, friendly, generous heart than on perfection. I've also discovered that hospitality does not have to find expression only within the four walls of a home.

Practice Out-of-the-House Hospitality

As much as I love Janice Peterson's definition of hospitality, I would tweak it just a bit to say: the welcoming reception and treatment of guests and strangers at home and out-of-the-house in a warm, friendly, generous way.

Hospitality

Hospitality certainly happens around a table in a kitchen, as it did when Bono visited the Petersons, but it also happens in a business meeting, at a conference, in a medical office, on the streets of a neighborhood, in a college dorm, in a hair salon . . .

Practicing out-of-the-house hospitality—noticing and welcoming the people I cross paths with every day—helps me take first steps in living connected.

I love this story my sister-in-law, Marianne, told me about practicing out-of-the-house hospitality with her young girls, Sarah and Faith.

> We took an old oatmeal can and brainstormed names of people we saw a lot—the librarian, the mailman, "Grandpa Bill" next door, the man we saw walking his dog every day, the lady at the nature center. Then we wrote those names on pieces of paper and put them in the can. We called it our "Special Person Jar." Then once a week, we would draw a name and do something for that person. We might give them something the girls made (like a tie-dyed butterfly bracelet made from a hair tie) or something they wrote. One day we put a cold pop in the mailbox for the mailman. We never bought gifts. We just used stuff we had or made things, including cards. The point was to let these people know they were special.[8]

One of those girls, Sarah, just went to college. She equipped her dorm room with a small refrigerator, a fabulous coffee maker, multiple pounds of coffee, various flavorings, and a variety of mugs. She frequently invites friends over for coffee.

Sarah, an introvert, clearly understands and values the joy of connecting with others, but she also understands that she does it best in her own quiet space rather than in a loud dining hall. What a great idea![9]

My introverted self wants to stay silent and enjoy my peaceful bubble, and sometimes I do, but I've discovered that every time I stretch to see and welcome another, whether in my home or outside my home, God refills my tank, just as He refilled the widow's jug with oil. And I learn things. I see the world differently through others' eyes. I laugh. And I find friends. Even in my neighborhood.

When we first moved into our new neighborhood, I felt overwhelmed. Our house needed a lot of attention inside and outside.

Just days after we moved into our house, a neighbor knocked on the door and invited me to a movie with some other neighbors. I declined because I felt so overwhelmed with the house that I knew I didn't have the energy to connect with new people. And I had never lived in a neighborhood where people offered those sorts of invitations.

Once we got the inside of the house painted, we moved to working on the outside. When I headed to the front gardens, I discovered that in this neighborhood, people do not often garden alone in the front yard. Within minutes, a neighbor wandered over, and we began a helpful conversation about perennials and weed control.

My neighbors kept stopping to chat, continued waving, and also kept organizing parties and offering us invitations.

They truly saw us and welcomed us in. Some of that welcome involved food, but much of it involved short conversations on a walk or in the front yard, a wave, a request for eggs, a request to buy cookies, and so on.

After living in this neighborhood more than twenty years, my husband and I laugh that we can't take a short walk. On a nice day, we run into at least two neighbors

Hospitality

who welcome a conversation. And I still can't garden solo in my front yard. I've come to so appreciate that.

I continue to learn that we introverts *can* do hospitality well, in a quiet, thoughtful way.

And we can, of course, learn from our extroverted friends.

For almost two decades I've had the same woman cutting my hair from her basement salon. I love what Patty does with my hair, but I also so admire the way she welcomes all sorts of people to her salon. One day during a haircut and color, I asked her how she learned to connect with so many people—about fifty every week. I know that I would feel utterly exhausted after cutting hair while also trying to talk to even two or three people.

> **Afton:** I think it is fabulous that you have all kinds of people in your chairs, and you find a way to talk with them. How do you do it?
> **Patty:** Some people talk more than others. I just draw them out with questions. I'm an extrovert, so to me it's not hard. I get more energy the more I talk, the more I'm down here.
> **Afton:** Do you take notes?
> **Patty:** No. I'm truly interested in their families. This is my forty-first year. I remember people from a long time ago. I remember their stories. And I don't remember stuff I'm supposed to remember. Ha!
> **Afton:** I'm sure you've heard some sad stories.
> **Patty:** Oh, yes. But I can usually make them feel better. My job is a happy job. Most people are looking forward to getting their hair done. They feel better when they leave.[10]

Patty even managed to get introverted me to talk. We've had some poignant conversations in that basement, conversations that built a friendship, one haircut at a time.

My admiration for what Patty does led me to think about how I can learn from her and adapt what she does to work with my introverted personality.

Three words stood out to me from my conversation with Patty: *interested, questions, remember*. And I've seen her live out these words with me, haircut after haircut.

I may not have it in me to cut hair and chat all day, but I certainly can find ways to show an *interest* in others. Everyone has a passion, and in true introverted fashion, I like to learn.

And I can come to events and situations with some *questions* already in my head, including questions about passions.

And I can cultivate the habit of *remembering* what people have told me by praying for them on my way to and from meeting with them. And then I can also remember to pray for them at home.

We introverts certainly don't have to become extroverts in order to cultivate friendships, but we can learn from extroverts and adapt their techniques in a way that works for our quiet, thoughtful selves. Admire and adapt. And we can thank God that He has wired us all differently.

> **Challenge Your Introverted Self**
> Interview an extroverted friend or family member who loves to practice hospitality.
> Ask about specific tips and techniques.
> Then sit down and write your introvert version of those tips and techniques. Pick one and try it at work or in your neighborhood or in your home. Keep notes about what worked and what didn't work.

Hospitality

In her thoughtful, challenging book *Invited: The Power of Hospitality in an Age of Loneliness*, author Leslie Verner offers such a clear vision for why hospitality matters: "Hospitality grips us by the chin and turns our face to notice, serve, and honor humanity inside, outside, and on the wayside. Sometimes we invite people into our homes and lives, and sometimes we go out and join people in unfamiliar or uncomfortable spaces. But we always pray for peeled-back eyes to walk our Jericho roads, seeing and celebrating the souls along the way as Jesus in disguise."[11]

Take some time now and work through the journaling questions and think about your own approach and attitude toward hospitality. Spend a few minutes asking God to open your eyes and heart to the gift of hospitality—at home and out-of-the-house.

And then, join me in the next chapter where we'll end our time together by talking about humility, an attitude that permeates genuine hospitality and also provides fuel for living connected.

Journaling Questions

1. What childhood memories do you associate with the word *hospitality*?
2. As an adult, what role has hospitality played in your life? Why?
3. Describe one in-house hospitality event that you enjoyed. Why?
4. Describe one out-of-the-house hospitality event that you enjoyed. Why?
5. Describe one hospitality event that went wacky. What did you learn from it?

6. What have you learned about hospitality from extroverted friends and family members?
7. Do you really believe that God will refill your introvert tank when you practice hospitality as a way of following God's command to "Love your neighbor as yourself"? Why or why not?

Chapter 12

Humility

Humility, as we all know, is one of those virtues that is never gained by seeking it. The more we pursue it the more distant it becomes. To think we have it is sure evidence that we don't.

—Richard J. Foster

Many years ago I had a brief conversation that I will forever associate with the word *humility*.

At the time, John worked for the radio station at Wheaton College. On this day, he told me that he would have a visitor in the WETN studio area—a man whom I greatly admired for his faith and writing: the Reverend John Stott. My husband invited me to pop in and say hello.

Yahoo!

I had heard Reverend Stott preach in London and also heard him speak in chapel at Wheaton College. His imposing stature and British accent drew me in immediately. But the more I listened, the more I heard something else that drew me in even more: his deep, deep love for Jesus. He had the ability to explain the complexities of faith and the life and death and resurrection of Jesus in a way that made intellectual sense and heart sense to me.

So, on that day, many years ago, I couldn't wait to meet my hero. Turned out our grade-school-aged son was home that day, so I brought him with me.

Living Connected

The two of us walked into the basement radio station lobby where I came face-to-face with the over six-foot-tall, kind-eyed Reverend John Stott.

I turned to our son and tried to explain to him why this man mattered so much. His words! His faith! What came out of my mouth was something like, "This is John Stott. He is a great man!"

Quickly and quietly, Reverend Stott smiled and shook his head: "Not a great man. Just a servant of God."

Those words came from a man named in the April 2005 issue of *TIME* magazine as one of the "100 Most Influential People." And the man who wrote more than fifty books. One of them—*Basic Christianity*—sold two million copies and was translated into more than sixty languages.[1]

When Reverend Stott died in 2011, the stories poured in with a common thread to my own story.[2]

> When I was nineteen I attended a day conference in Newcastle at which John Stott was the speaker. When we arrived, the friend with whom I'd come went off to the toilet and I was left alone, feeling out of place. An older man came over and began talking to me, asking me about myself. After a few moments my friend returned and the man introduced himself, "Hello, I'm John Stott."[3]

How would our world, our relationships change if humility (down-to-earthness, modesty, freedom from pride or arrogance[4]) swept over us?

Focus Our Eyes and Minds on Others

We introverts love to think and read and mess with words and ideas. Our heads provide such a cozy, imaginative environment. Why leave that comfortable, life-giving place? Why set our minds to thinking of others? Why train our eyes to see, truly see, others?

Because God calls us to it.

I love the way the apostle Paul explains that call. And I love the way that Eugene Peterson translated Paul's words into everyday language.

> If you've gotten anything at all out of following Christ, if his love has made any difference in your life, if being in a community of the Spirit means anything to you, if you have a heart, if you *care*—then do me a favor: Agree with each other, love each other, be deep-spirited friends. Don't push your way to the front; don't sweet-talk your way to the top. Put yourself aside, and help others get ahead. Don't be obsessed with getting your own advantage. Forget yourselves long enough to lend a helping hand. (Philippians 2:1–4 MSG)

So how do we stop our self-obsession and forget ourselves long enough to reach for others who need us? Clearly, we can't just wake up one morning and decide, *From today onward I shall become humble.* We can, however, develop some habits that will lead the way, including service.

Find Ways to Serve

We can so easily get caught up in the to-do list part of serving: help this person, help that person, do this, do that . . . That approach, as we talked about in other chapters, generates exhaustion and fosters unequal, unhealthy relationships where one person functions solely as the giver.

What if our serving focused instead on not-so-visible acts, such as listening, seeing, and praying—all activities that suit our introverted selves so well.

We can listen.

Everyone has a story that needs telling, and we introverts like to listen. We can't heal diseases or broken hearts as Jesus did, but we certainly can offer the healing balm of a good listen.

Author Adam McHugh in his book *The Listening Life* thoughtfully explains the tie-in between listening and humility.

> A commitment to listening is one of the best antidotes for power and privilege. A servant listener does not dominate the conversation. Servants take the attention off themselves and focus their attention on the needs and interests of others. . . . Servant listening is a practice of presence, in which we set aside what might distract us and what we think should happen in a moment or conversation. It is an act of humility, in which we acknowledge that no matter who we are listening to, we come to learn.[5]

We can see and acknowledge each person we encounter daily.

We introverts tend to notice things and people others might miss. We can embrace that ability and work to get out of our heads and acknowledge those around us, no matter their race or station, without even using words. A smile and a wave all communicate (at least in my Western culture), *I see you.*

Humility

While writing this chapter on humility all wrapped up in serving, I remembered a story about a professor who, because of His love for God, continually stepped out of his academic role to see and connect with people, including the homeless. His seeing and connecting then compelled him to compassionate action. I asked his widow to tell me more about her husband's serving heart.

> He always had a heart for people who were estranged for some reason or another—people who lost their home, their job, were down on their luck . . . He just seemed to have an awareness of people, probably from his studying. He really cared about people who were outsiders.
>
> He made it a point to talk to the homeless people in our city. He knew them by name. And he met with our mayor several times to talk about how to help them. That began a process that eventually resulted in the building of a shelter.[6]

> **Introvert Inclinations**
> Enjoy doing quiet, useful tasks others might not enjoy.
> Carefully observe people and situations.
> Enjoy silence, even in the presence of other people.

We can pray, asking God to make us more like Him.

As I've written in almost every chapter, prayer suits the introverted soul so well. And God says it matters. What if we prayed this prayer every morning as we began our daily routine?

> Dear God, give me your eyes to see and your ears to hear. Help me this day to be your hands and feet to those I meet.

Throughout His short life on this earth, Jesus continually reached for people, and they reached for Him.

> One day some parents brought their children to Jesus so he could touch and bless them. But the disciples scolded the parents for bothering him. When Jesus saw what was happening, he was angry with his disciples. He said to them, "Let the children come to me. Don't stop them! For the Kingdom of God belongs to those who are like these children. I tell you the truth, anyone who doesn't receive the Kingdom of God like a child will never enter it." Then he took the children in his arms and placed his hands on their heads and blessed them. (Mark 10:13–16)

Jesus truly saw people and heard their hearts with no regard to their age, race, or social status.

Why do we get so wrapped up in what *we* want and need and think and often few people as a bother? Perhaps pride has a lot to do with it.

Wrestle with Pride

In the play *King Lear* by William Shakespeare, the main character, the aging king of Britain, spends most of the play not seeing the real drama in his own family or the real drama within his own heart. The Earl of Gloucester does the same until villains pluck out his eyes. Suddenly, when he can no longer physically see, he *can* truly see and understand both his situation and himself. He understands his pride and mistakes: "I stumbled when I saw."[7] And he speaks aloud his need of forgiveness.

As the play progresses, Lear and Gloucester begin truly to see, and Lear also asks for forgiveness: "You must bear with me. Pray you now, forget and forgive: I am old and foolish."[8]

Humility

As Shakespeare's tragedies all do, *King Lear* ends with sorrow—a pile of broken relationships and destroyed lives. And the reader (watcher) can't help but wonder, *What would have happened if Lear and Gloucester had found their true eyesight earlier? What if they had adopted a stance of humility rather than self-serving pride earlier in their stories? What if they had learned as young men to say, "Please, forgive me"?*

Imagine what might happen in our world, around a dinner table, across a boardroom, on social media, in a neighborhood, in churches, or in school hallways if we rolled up our sleeves and committed ourselves to practicing humility by admitting our mistakes and asking for forgiveness! I think we would find ourselves in a world with more joy and less anxiety. Maybe even a more connected, less lonely world.

Lear and Gloucester did not "see" truly until physical tragedy struck their lives. So often this happens with us too—tragedy flattens us, removing any puffed-up air we might have had. But we do not need to wait for life to shake the pride out of us.

We can address our pride by granting a trusted friend (or two) permission to "call us out."

As I worked on this book, I gathered a team of people around me, whom I dubbed "early readers." I asked these people to speak honestly to me. I wanted to know what they thought didn't work, what they thought did work, and what they thought needed rewriting or reorganizing. I know that when I write I can get so lost in my head that I don't communicate clearly or helpfully. I needed this accountability.

And I need a similar accountability in life. I need people who call me out when I don't live well, whether that means holding a grudge, getting hyperfocused on my own stuff, or forgetting to see, really see, the people I interact with every day.

How fortunate I feel to have a spouse with whom I can have these sorts of honest discussions.

> **Introvert Impediments**
> Can live so much in their heads that they become excessively self-focused.
> Can tend toward self-reliance rather than humbly seeking support and help from God and from friends.
> Can tend toward comparison with extroverts and feel inadequate rather than seeing introversion as a connection-building gift.

We can address our pride by practicing the Daily Examen.

I have come to love this five-hundred-year-old daily spiritual practice, something I try to do at the end of most days before I drift off to sleep. Mark Thibodeaux, a spiritual director for Jesuits, provides a simple guideline:

- Give thanksgiving to God for all that happened in the day.
- Ask God to fill me with His Spirit and give me His eyes to evaluate my day.
- Review and acknowledge my failures.
- Ask God for forgiveness and healing related to those failures.
- Invite God to show up in the events of the next day by naming each event.[9]

Humility

We can address our pride by practicing silence.

We introverts, who love silence, know so well how staying quiet can save us from so many awkward foot-in-mouth situations. But staying silent can also act as a way to practice humility and thus encourage others and ultimately lay the foundation for a connection. This story says it so well.

> In my husband's work environment, people like to be the smartest in the room and use every opportunity to show that they are the smartest. That really bothers my husband, and he doesn't want to be that way.
>
> My husband is a brilliant man, and he has many opportunities to show that he is, yet time and time again I see him holding his tongue, being gracious in silence. Over and over. He never wants someone to feel stupid or embarrassed.
>
> This has translated into our relationship as well. In twenty-seven years of marriage, he has never taken joy in making me feel stupid, though I have given him many opportunities! He graciously covers and supports me.
>
> One time I miscalculated the time between our daughter's driving permit and the time she could get her license. So my daughter and I got up early, got over to the DMV, and found out that we were there a month early.
>
> My husband was so gracious and kind. I was crying because I felt so dumb. He was beyond kind.
>
> This kind of humility is beautiful to experience and witness.[10]

> **Challenge Your Introverted Self**
>
> Do you have someone in your life who will "call you out" when you get too wrapped up in yourself? If not, who could you talk to about becoming this person in your life? Could you meet once a month and both answer this question: How did my self-absorption keep me from reaching for others?

Reach for People Because of Jesus

When people who love Jesus reach for others, they change the world by filling it with hope and joy—one person at a time.

My friend Jody watched this kind of living play out with her father in his last days.

> Dad had a heart for people no matter who they were. This humbleness of heart became magnified in the last years of his life.
>
> As Dad grew more elderly, his world grew increasingly narrow. He was committed to walking with Mom as she journeyed down Alzheimer's confusing dark path. During Dad's last year and a half, this meant rising early in the morning and making the slow trek from his apartment building to the connecting nursing facility. He would arrive in time to have breakfast with Mom and spend the next twelve to thirteen hours by her side until she was safely tucked into bed for the night.
>
> Though the landscape of my dad's daily life had changed, Dad had not. The people at this nursing home now became "his people." He knew them and greeted them by name, from the teenager working as wait staff to the cleaning lady who vacuumed the carpet, from the CPN who dressed my mom to the nurse who came with medicines, from the elderly resident who put together puzzles in the hallway, to the spouse of the patient down the hall who needed an encouraging word, and even the maintenance man who came to fix the heater. In his quiet way, he listened to them, cared about them, encouraged them, and prayed for them. He loved them, and they knew it.
>
> In the final weeks of his life, a fast-growing cancer ravaged his body. Dad went from being a daily caregiver to being a patient in need of care.
>
> As the final hours of his life here on earth drew near, a steady stream of "his people" flowed in and out of the room to say goodbye. With tear-filled eyes, they thanked him for his friendship.

Humility

> While Dad is now home in heaven, the rippling effects of the joy of his simple, caring ways still linger in the lives of those he loved. His was a quiet ministry of humble friendship that impacted the lives of those in his world for Jesus's sake.[11]

Oh, may we leave such a legacy—a legacy of seeing, hearing, caring. A legacy of humility. A legacy of connection.

And none of this reaching means turning ourselves inside-out to live as extroverts. Instead, it means thanking God for His good gift of introversion and celebrating and using the connection abilities we already have as a result of this gift.

I keep a quotation from Adam McHugh's book *Introverts in the Church* on my dresser so that I see it every morning. His friend Veronica said, "I'd like to think that the work of God might be displayed through my introversion, and not in spite of it."[12]

Yes, oh, yes!

Let us cheer each other on as we seek to live connected in a quiet, thoughtful sort of way!

Dear God, please help these readers to rejoice in the ways you have wired and gifted them. Grant them courage to share themselves with others. And shower them with deep, deep joy in the journey.

Amen.

Journaling Questions

1. Who do you think of when you think of the word *humility?*
2. With which aspect of practicing humility do you struggle most—recognizing and addressing

pride, learning to set aside your own wants and needs for the sake of another when it feels inconvenient to do that, trying to "do, do, do" your way into humble service, staying silent and letting another have center stage, or something else?
3. Imagine a world where people routinely said, "Please, forgive me." What do you think would happen to our relationships, businesses, politics?
4. Have you experienced the challenge of an accountability relationship? How did it begin? How did it help? What impact did it have on your other relationships?
5. How does practicing humility fit in with using the gifts and talents God has given you?
6. What about Jesus? What did He do in his short life on this earth that impresses you? What did He do that challenges you? If He chose to live humbly on this earth, what does that say to you?
7. When you leave this earth, what stories do you hope people will tell about you? How might you tweak the way you live now in light of that hope?

What Now?

As you close the pages of this book, may you go into your world with courage and hope to pursue living connected.

May you rejoice in your quiet voice as a gift from God.

May you remember that others need to hear your quiet voice.

May you experience the joy of walking with God through the always challenging process of living connected.

May you find friends. And deepen the friendships you already have.

How I wish that we could sit in my quiet backyard with a cup of coffee and talk about living connected. I know that I would learn so much from you. And you know I love to hear stories! Although we may not meet face-to-face, please know that I would love to connect with you online.

Website: https://aftonrorvik.com/
Twitter: @AftonRorvik, https://twitter.com/AftonRorvik
Facebook: @LearningtoLiveConnected, https://www.facebook.com/LearningtoLiveConnected/
Goodreads: https://www.goodreads.com/author/show/2845576.Afton_Rorvik

Notes

Introduction

1. Adam S. McHugh, *Introverts in the Church: Finding Our Place in an Extroverted Culture* (Downers Grove, IL: InterVarsity Press, 2017), loc. 487 of 3337, Kindle.

1. Honesty

1. Email correspondence with the author, January 14, 2018, and January 24, 2021.
2. John Townsend, *How to Be a Best Friend Forever: Making and Keeping Lifetime Relationships* (Nashville: Worthy, 2011), loc. 509-516 of 1445, Kindle.
3. Susan Cain, *Quiet: The Power of Introverts in a World That Can't Stop Talking* (New York: Broadway Paperbacks, 2013), 11.
4. This quiz can get you started: "5 Love Languages Quiz," https://www.5lovelanguages.com/quizzes/.
5. Dorothy Littell Greco, *Making Marriage Beautiful: Lifelong Love, Joy, and Intimacy Start with You* (Colorado Springs: David C. Cook, 2017), loc. 451-462 of 3004, Kindle.
6. Michael Barbaro, "A Special Episode for Kids: The Fear Facer," September 29, 2019, *The Daily*, produced by Julia Longoria, podcast, 31:08, https://www.nytimes.com/2019/09/29/podcasts/the-daily/children-fears-ocd-anxiety.html?.

2. Generosity

1. "What Is Generosity?" University of Notre Dame Science of Generosity © 2017, accessed Feb. 3, 2018. http://

generosityresearch.nd.edu/more-about-the-initiative/what-is-generosity/.
2. Frances Hodgson Burnett, *A Little Princess: Being the Whole Story of Sara Crewe Now Being Told for the First Time* (New York: HarperFestival, 1963), 80.
3. Merriam-Webster, s.v. "generosity," accessed January 26, 2021, https://www.merriam-webster.com/thesaurus/generosity.
4. Quoted from Karen Kleiman, "Are You an Over-Giver?," *Psychology Today*, March 26, 2014, https://www.psychologytoday.com/blog/isnt-what-i-expected/201403/are-you-over-giver-1.
5. Afton Rorvik, "I discovered this yesterday in a wet parking lot near Dunkin Donuts with no one in sight." Facebook, December 18, 2017, www.facebook.com/LearningtoLiveConnected/posts/1654331201318226.
6. Carlene Hill Byron, email correspondence with the author, April 24, 2018.
7. John Rorvik, email correspondence with the author, December 2, 2020.
8. Lisa-Jo Baker, *Never Unfriended: The Secret to Finding and Keeping Lasting Friendships* (Nashville: B&H Publishing, 2017), 71.
9. April Yamasaki, *Four Gifts: Seeking Self-Care for Heart, Soul, Mind, and Strength* (Harrisburg, VA: Herald Press, 2018), loc. 326 and 309 of 2295, Kindle.

3. Approachability

1. Susan Cain, *Quiet: The Power of Introverts in a World That Can't Stop Talking* (New York: Broadway Paperbacks, 2013), 11.
2. WordHippo, s.v. "approachability," https://www.wordhippo.com/what-is/another-word-for/approachability.html.
3. Email correspondence with the author, January 6, 2021.
4. Joe Navarro with Marvin Karlins, *What Every Body Is Saying: An Ex-FBI Agent's Guide to Speed-Reading People* (New York: HarperCollins, 2008), 1–2.

Notes

5. "Smile and Wave . . . or Maybe Not: Reflections on Greetings Around the World," International Writers' Blog, Brown University, November 9, 2014, https://blogs.brown.edu/international-writers/2014/11/09/greetings-around-the-world-2/.
6. Joe Navarro, *The Dictionary of Body Language: A Field Guide to Human Behavior* (New York: HarperCollins, 2018), loc. 1014 of 2221, Kindle.
7. Lauraine Snelling, Facebook, https://www.facebook.com/lauraine.snelling.
8. Abraham Lincoln to General Ulysses S. Grant on July 13, 1863, *Collected Works of Abraham Lincoln. Volume 6* (The Abraham Lincoln Association), 326, https://quod.lib.umich.edu/l/lincoln/lincoln6/1:689?rgn=div1;view=fulltext.
9. Nelson, *Frientimacy*, loc. 1749 of 4405, Kindle.

4. Curiosity

1. Brian Grazer, *A Curious Mind: The Secret to a Bigger Life* (New York: Simon and Schuster, 2015), 24.
2. William Shakespeare, *Much Ado about Nothing*, 5.1.134-136 (act, scene, and line), in Bertrand Evans, ed., *The College Shakespeare: 15 Plays and the Sonnets* (New York: Macmillan Publishing Co., 1973), 275.
3. "The Interesting Meaning and History of the Phrase 'Curiosity Killed the Cat,'" Interesting Literature, December 2, 2019, https://interestingliterature.com/2019/12/meaning-and-history-phrase-curiosity-killed-the-cat/.
4. Email correspondence with the author, April 17, 2020.
5. Mario Livio, *Why?: What Makes Us Curious* (New York: Simon and Schuster, 2017), 172.
6. Augustine, *Confessions*, trans. Albert C. Outler (Dallas: Southern Methodist University, 1955), book 11, chapter 12 (emphasis mine).
7. H. A. Rey, *Curious George Takes a Job* (Boston: Houghton Mifflin Company, 1975), 47.

8. Jill Suttie, "Why Curious People Have Better Relationships," *Greater Good Magazine* (Greater Good Science Center at UC Berkeley), May 31, 2017, https://greatergood.berkeley.edu/article/item/why_curious_people_have_better_relationships.
9. Todd Kashdan, *Curious? Discover the Missing Ingredient to a Fulfilling Life* (New York: HarperCollins, 2009), 135.
10. Falecia Sanchez, conversation with the author, April 22, 2020.
11. John Rorvik, conversation with the author, July 8, 2020.
12. Adam S. McHugh, *The Listening Life: Embracing Attentiveness in a World of Distraction* (Downers Grove, IL: InterVarsity Press, 2015), loc. 1905 of 3214, Kindle.
13. Ilana Kowarski, "What Is the Socratic Method That Law Schools Use?" *US News and World Report*, April 4, 2019, https://www.usnews.com/education/best-graduate-schools/top-law-schools/articles/2019-04-04/what-is-the-socratic-method-and-why-do-law-schools-use-it.
14. Grazer, *A Curious Mind*, 261.
15. Lara Krupinka, email correspondence with the author, July 23, 2020.

5. Empathy

1. Belinda Bauman, *Brave Souls: Experiencing the Audacious Power of Empathy* (Downers Grove, Illinois: InterVarsity Press, 2019), loc. 727-733 of 3278, Kindle, emphasis mine.
2. Email correspondence with the author, May 7, 2020.
3. Sesame Street, "Les Mousserables (Les Mis Parody)," March 7, 2014, youtube.com/watch?v=GyYZfSmwH3c&feature=youtu.be.
4. Daniel J. Siegel, *Mindsight: The New Science of Personal Transformation* (New York: Bantam Books, 2010), loc. 1161-1178 of 5288, Kindle.
5. Tom Frens, email correspondence with the author, May 18, 2020.

Notes

6. Judith Orloff, "9 Self-Protection Strategies for Empaths," Quiet Revolution (blog), https://www.quietrev.com/9-self-protection-strategies-for-empaths/.
7. Adam S. McHugh, *Introverts in the Church: Finding Our Place in an Extroverted Culture*, rev. ed. (Downers Grove, Illinois: InterVarsity Press, 2017), 67.

6. Loyalty

1. Merriam-Webster, s.v. "loyalty (kids definition)," merriam-webster.com/dictionary/loyalty.
2. Roberta Choma, email correspondence with the author, July 2020. Story used by permission.
3. Felton, *Loyalty: That Vexing Virtue* (New York: Simon and Schuster Paperbacks, 2011), loc. 1947 of 4433, Kindle, emphasis mine.
4. Adapted from Timothy Keiningham, Lerzan Aksoy, and Luke Williams, *Why Loyalty Matters: The Groundbreaking Approach to Rediscovering Happiness, Meaning, and Lasting Fulfillment in Your Life and Work* (Dallas: BenBella Books, 2009), 130.
5. Shasta Nelson, *The Business of Friendship: Making the Most of Our Relationships Where We Spend Most of Our Time* (New York: HarperCollins Leadership, 2020), 52–53.
6. Email correspondence and phone calls with the author, July 2020.
7. Stephen R. Covey, "Be Loyal to Those Absent," Franklin Covey (blog), https://resources.franklincovey.com/franklincovey-blog/be-loyal-to-those-absent.
8. Email correspondence with the author, August 4, 2020.
9. Dr. John Townsend, *How to Be a Best Friend Forever: Making and Keeping Lifetime Relationships* (Brentwood, TN: Worthy Publishing, 2011), 96.
10. Email correspondence with the author, May 2020.
11. Email correspondence and phone calls with the author, June and July 2020.
12. Jody Lubenec, texts with the author, July 29, 2020.

7. Confidentiality

1. Oxford Lexico, s.v. "confidentiality," https://www.lexico.com/definition/confidentiality.
2. "Health Insurance Portability and Accountability Act of 1996 (HIPAA)," Centers for Disease Control and Prevention (CDC), September 14, 2018, cdc.gov/phlp/publications/topic/hipaa.html.
3. Merriam-Webster, s.v. "breach of confidentiality," https://www.merriam-webster.com/dictionary/breach%20of%20confidentiality.
4. Jennifer Stenzel, interview with the author, September 9, 2020.
5. Joseph Epstein, *Gossip: The Untrivial Pursuit* (Boston: Mariner Books, 2011), 20.
6. Email correspondence with the author, December 18, 2021.
7. Mark Galli and David Goetz, "Amazing Grace-Filled Gossip: An Interview with Author Kathleen Norris," *Christianity Today: CT Pastors*, January 1, 1999, https://www.christianitytoday.com/pastors/1999/winter/9l1056.html.
8. Jacqui Harmeling, email correspondence with the author, September 5, 2020.
9. Email correspondence with the author, October 1, 2020.
10. Cal Newport, *Digital Minimalism: Choosing a Focused Life in a Noisy World* (New York: Portfolio/Penguin, 2019), 28.
11. Peggy Ingram, email correspondence with the author, November 18, 2020.

8. Consistency

1. Email correspondence with the author, November 15–16, 2020.
2. Merriam-Webster, s.v. "consistency," https://www.merriam-webster.com/dictionary/consistency.

Notes

3. James Clear, "How Long Does It Actually Take to Form a New Habit? (Backed by Science)," *3-2-1* Thursday newsletter, https://jamesclear.com/new-habit.
4. James Clear, *Atomic Habits: An Easy & Proven Way to Build Good Habits & Break Bad Ones* (New York: Avery, 2018), loc. 113-149 of 4551, Kindle.
5. Clear, *Atomic Habits*, loc. 419 of 4551, Kindle.
6. Email correspondence with the author, September 27, 2020.
7. Clear, *Atomic Habits*, loc. 969 of 4551, Kindle.
8. Alan Loy McGinnis, *The Friendship Factor: How to Get Closer to the People You Care For* (Minneapolis: Augsburg Fortress, 2004), loc. 2280-2293 of 2826, Kindle.
9. Email correspondence with the author, June 8, 2020. Story used by permission.
10. John Rorvik, email correspondence with the author, December 1, 2020. Story used by permission.
11. Donald Miller, "StoryBrand Productivity Schedule," 2017, https://storybrand.com/downloads/StoryBrand_Productivity_Schedule.pdf.
12. Peggy Ingram, email correspondence with the author, November 2020. Story used by permission.

9. Flexibility

1. Text messages, Friday, November 6, 2020; Tuesday, November 10, 2020; and Thursday, November 19, 2020. Used by permission.
2. Dictionary.com, s.v. "flexibility," https://www.dictionary.com/browse/flexibility.
3. "Benefits of Flexibility Exercises," Harvard Health Publishing, Harvard Medical School, April 2015, www.health.harvard.edu/staying-healthy/benefits-of-flexibility-exercises.
4. Chris R. Mazzarella, phone interview with the author, January 15, 2021.

5. Shasta Nelson, "The Gift of Flexibility in Relationships," Girl Friend Circles (blog), August 28, 2015. girlfriendcircles.com/blog/index.php/2015/08/flexibility-relationships-compromise.
6. Melody Copenny, email correspondence with the author, January 7, 2021. Used by permission.
7. Mary Schmich, "Advice, Like Youth, Probably Just Wasted on the Young," *Chicago Tribune*, June 1, 1997, https://www.chicagotribune.com/columns/chi-schmich-sunscreen-column-column.html.
8. Susan David, PhD, *Emotional Agility: Get Unstuck, Embrace Change, and Thrive in Work and Life* (New York: Penguin Random House, LLC, 2016), loc. 103-110 of 4486, Kindle.
9. Ellen Rorvik, email correspondence with the author, January 5, 2021. Used by permission.
10. Email correspondence with the author, January 5, 2021. Used by permission.
11. Sharla Fritz, email correspondence with the author, December 10, 2020.
12. Sharon Garlough Brown, *Sensible Shoes: A Story about the Spiritual Journey* (Downers Grove, IL: InterVarsity Press, 2013), 289–90.

10. Creativity

1. Suzanne Alexander, email correspondence with the author, January 17, 2021.
2. Luci Shaw, *Breath for the Bones: Art, Imagination, and Spirit* (Nashville: Thomas Nelson, 2007), 112.
3. These are the opening words to almost every movie in the *Star Wars* saga.
4. Homer, *The Odyssey: The Story of Odysseus*, translated by W. H. D. Rouse (New York: New American Library, 1937), 11.
5. Eugene H. Peterson, *Leap Over a Wall* (New York: HarperOne, 1997), 3-4.

Notes

6. Maria Alexandra Vettese and Stephanie Congdon Barnes, *A Year Between Friends 3191 Miles Apart: Crafts, Recipes, Letter, and Stories* (New York: Abrams, 2016), loc. 23-51 of 1788, Kindle.
7. Jayne and her family run Homeland Creamery in Julian, North Carolina. https://www.homelandcreamery.com/about.
8. Jayne Wilson Bowman, conversation and email with the author in 2019 and on January 20, 2021.
9. Shaw, *Breath for the Bones*, 112.
10. Susan Cain, *Quiet: The Power of Introverts in a World That Can't Stop Talking* (New York: Broadway Paperbacks, 2013), 11.
11. Leslie Verner, *Invited: The Power of Hospitality in an Age of Loneliness* (Harrisonburg, VA: Herald Press, 2019), loc. 207-214 of 2754, Kindle.
12. Sheila Wise Rowe, *Healing Racial Trauma: The Road to Resilience* (Downer's Grove, IL: InterVarsity Press, 2020), loc. 2343 of 3027, Kindle.

11. Hospitality

1. Nilwona Nowlin, email correspondence with the author, January 28, 2021. See more about Nilwona's workshops at http://nilwona.com/.
2. Janice Peterson, *Becoming Gertrude: How Our Friendships Shape Our Faith* (Colorado Springs: NavPress, 2018), loc. 873 of 1334, Kindle.
3. *Bono and Eugene Peterson: The Psalms*, directed by Nathan Clarke, April 26, 2016, Fuller Studio, Fuller Theological Seminary, https://www.youtube.com/watch?v=-140S5e90KY.
4. Jen Schmidt, *Just Open the Door: How One Invitation Can Change a Generation* (Nashville: B&H Publishing Group, 2018), loc. 210-221 of 3242, Kindle.
5. Tom Frens, email correspondence with the author, January 28, 2021.

6. Dorothy Greco, email correspondence with the author, January 19, 2021.
7. JoHannah Reardon, "Hospitality for Introverts: How Can You Practice Hospitality When You'd Rather Be Alone?" *Today's Christian Woman*, May 2010, todayschristianwoman.com/articles/2010/may/hospitalityintroverts.html.
8. Marianne Talmage, phone conversation with the author, January 28, 2021.
9. Sarah Talmage, email correspondence with the author, January 30, 2021.
10. Patty Spence, interview with the author, January 28, 2021.
11. Leslie Verner, *Invited: The Power of Hospitality in an Age of Loneliness* (Harrisonburg, VA: Herald Press, 2019), loc. 853-859 of 2754, Kindle.

12. Humility

1. Billy Graham, "Heroes & Icons: John Stott," *TIME Magazine*, April 14, 2005, http://content.time.com/time/specials/packages/article/0,28804,1972656_1972717_1974108,00.html.
2. Chris Norton, compiler, "Leaders and Friends Remember John Stott," *Christianity Today*, July 29, 2011, https://www.christianitytoday.com/ct/2011/julyweb-only/johnstottroundup.html.
3. Tim Chester, "The First Time I Met John Stott," blog post, July 28, 2011, https://timchester.wordpress.com/2011/07/28/the-first-time-i-met-john-stott/.
4. Merriam-Webster, s.v. "humility," https://www.merriam-webster.com/dictionary/humility.
5. Adam S. McHugh, *The Listening Life: Embracing Attentiveness in a World of Distraction* (Downers Grove, IL: InterVarsity Press, 2015), loc. 199 of 3214, Kindle.
6. Email correspondence with the author, February 9, 2021. Used by permission.

Notes

7. William Shakespeare, *King Lear*, 4.1.21 (act, scene, and line), in Bertrand Evans, ed., *The College Shakespeare: 15 Plays and the Sonnets* (New York: Macmillan Publishing Co., 1973), 543.
8. Shakespeare, *King Lear*, 4.7.85, in Evans, *College Shakespeare*, 553.
9. Mark Thibodeaux, "Try the Daily Examen," Loyola Press, https://www.loyolapress.com/catholic-resources/ignatian-spirituality/examen-and-ignatian-prayer/how-can-i-pray-try-the-daily-examen/?utm_source=ignsp&utm_medium=blog&utm_campaign=ignatian.
10. Email correspondence with the author, February 10, 2021. Story used by permission.
11. Jody Lubenec, email correspondence with the author, February 7, 2021.
12. Adam S. McHugh, *Introverts in the Church: Finding Our Place in an Extroverted Culture* (Downers Grove, IL: InterVarsity Press, 2017), 54.

Resources

I discovered and rediscovered a lot of book friends in the process of writing this book. I've listed some of them here in the thought that you might also want to befriend one or two of them.

Becoming Gertrude: How Our Friendships Shape Our Faith by Janice Peterson

The Business of Friendship: Making the Most of Our Relationships Where We Spend Most of Our Time by Shasta Nelson

Celebration of Discipline: The Path to Spiritual Growth by Richard J. Foster

Digital Minimalism: Choosing a Focused Life in a Noisy World by Cal Newport

Emotional Agility: Get Unstuck, Embrace Change, and Thrive in Work and Life by Susan David

The Emotionally Healthy Woman: Eight Things You Have to Quit to Change Your Life by Geri Scazzero

The Freedom of Self-Forgetfulness: The Path to True Christian Joy by Timothy Keller

Four Gifts: Seeking Self-Care for Heart, Soul, Mind, and Strength by April Yamasaki

Living Connected

The Friendship Factor: How to Get Closer to the People You Care For by Alan Loy McGinnis

Frientimacy: How to Deepen Friendships for Lifelong Health and Happiness by Shasta Nelson

How to Be a Best Friend Forever: Making and Keeping Lifetime Relationships by John Townsend

Introverts in the Church: Finding Our Place in an Extroverted Culture by Adam S. McHugh

Invited: The Power of Hospitality in an Age of Loneliness by Leslie Verner

The Listening Life: Embracing Attentiveness in a World of Distraction by Adam S. McHugh

Leap Over a Wall: Earthy Spirituality for Everyday Christians by Eugene H. Peterson

Loyalty: The Vexing Virtue by Eric Felten

Making Marriage Beautiful: Lifelong Love, Joy, and Intimacy Start with You by Dorothy Littell Greco

Marriage in the Middle: Embracing Midlife Surprises, Challenges, and Joys by Dorothy Littell Greco

Mindsight: The New Science of Personal Transformation by Daniel J. Siegel

The Powerful Purpose of Introverts: Why the World Needs YOU to BE YOU by Holley Gerth

Resources

Quiet: The Power of Introverts in a World That Can't Stop Talking by Susan Cain

The Road to Character by David Brooks

Sensible Shoes series by Sharon Garlough Brown

Walking on Water: Reflections of Faith and Art by Madeleine L'Engle

If you enjoyed this book, will you consider sharing
the message with others?

Let us know your thoughts. You can let the author know by visiting or sharing a photo of the cover on our social media pages or leaving a review at a retailer's site. All of it helps us get the message out!

Email: info@ironstreammedia.com

   @ironstreammedia

Brookstone Publishing Group, Harambee Press, Iron Stream, Iron Stream Fiction, Iron Stream Kids, and Life Bible Study are imprints of Iron Stream Media, which derives its name from Proverbs 27:17, "As iron sharpens iron, so one person sharpens another." This sharpening describes the process of discipleship, one to another. With this in mind, Iron Stream Media provides a variety of solutions for churches, ministry leaders, and nonprofits ranging from in-depth Bible study curriculum and Christian book publishing to custom publishing and consultative services.

For more information on ISM and its imprints, please visit
IronStreamMedia.com

www.ingramcontent.com/pod-product-compliance
Lightning Source LLC
Chambersburg PA
CBHW070530090426
42735CB00013B/2935